Three of the Best

CANDACE LEWIS is a lawyer and legal author who has worked in private practice, publishing and consultancy. She has an Arts/Law degree and a Master of Laws, with honours, in consumer protection, trade practices and family law. Candace is also a qualified personal trainer and is passionate about fitness for women. She has two children.

MARGARET O'SULLIVAN was a staff journalist for more than 20 years, working on *The Sydney Morning Herald*, *Sun-Herald*, *Woman's Day* and *The Australian Women's Weekly*. She also wrote book columns for *Good Housekeeping*, the *Sun-Herald*, and *Elle* magazine.

She is the author of four cookbooks, *Jams, Jellies and Marmalades*, *Mustards, Pickles and Chutneys*, *Divine Desserts* and *Perfect Picnics*. All were published in the US and Canada as well as Australia. She is also the author of a diet book, *The Heavenly Body Diet*.

Candace Lewis &
Margaret O'Sullivan

Three of the Best

the **modern
woman's
guide** to
everything

ABC
Books

Published by ABC Books for the
AUSTRALIAN BROADCASTING CORPORATION
GPO Box 9994 Sydney NSW 2001

First published December 2008
Reprinted January 2009

Lewis, Candace, 1961–
   Three of the best : the modern woman's guide to everything
   / Candace Lewis, Margaret O'Sullivan.
   1st ed.
   ISBN 978 0 7333 2364 5 (pbk.)
   Women — Health and hygiene.
   Beauty, Personal.
   Self-management (Psychology) for women.
   O'Sullivan, Margaret.
646.7

Cover and internal design by Jane Cameron, Fisheye Design
Illustrations by Ian Faulkner
Typeset in 11.5 on 14pt Mrs Eaves by Kirby Jones
Printed by Quality Printing, Hong Kong, China

10 9 8 7 6 5 4 3 2

To my Three of the Best —
Peter, Maxwell and Pascale
CL

To my Three of the Best —
Jean, Teresa and Erina
MO'S

The authors would like to thank:

Alison Gordon
Vicki Tillott
Peter Mann
Australian Society of Plastic Surgeons
Australasian College of Dermatologists

CONTENTS

INTRODUCTION

Why *Three of the Best?* Because every day we are faced with numerous choices. We go to the supermarket and find shopping aisles overflowing with breakfast cereals. If we go to a sandwich bar for lunch we confront a wall of possible combinations. When we go shopping for bathroom tiles there are literally tens of thousands to choose from. There are 15 whites in a paint colour chart, and that's before customised mixing.

All this, you would think, is making us happy. However recent research suggests otherwise. While some choice is good, too much leaves us bewildered and frustrated. Many of us now crave a simpler life with the choice of, say, three fruit juice options, not 30. With a choice of 30, instead of enjoying the watermelon juice, you spend the next ten minutes wondering if you should have had the guava with ginger. You worry about what you may have missed out on rather than enjoying the decision you made.

As consumers we often feel out of control and time-poor in the face of an information avalanche. We read newspapers and magazines and often come across scraps of information that it would be useful to cut out and keep. But who has the time?

Most of us have good intentions. We want to be healthier in mind, body and soul, but how to start? If we spend too much time thinking about the best way to take those first steps we may not take them at all. It might just seem too hard.

Three of the Best brings together a wealth of information in an easy-to-access format. It presents three top choices in most areas of life where choices have to be made.

Because we've covered a lot of ground, you may not need to know it all. To make the information you need to know easily accessible, we've divided the book into seven sections covering major areas of life. Do you want a flat stomach or firm upper arms? You'll find Three of the Best steps in the FIT section. Need to whiten your teeth? You'll find Three of the Best ways (at home and professionally) in BEAUTIFUL, along with the latest research on staying youthful and tips on make-up. PEACE is about calmness of mind and covers all the areas that help to create that, such as meditation, relaxation, decluttering and pathways to happiness. STAND UP, SURVIVAL, FUEL and DOWNTIME, give information on your rights, first-aid, food and fun. Don't know what to do when you are facing separation or what your legal position is when divorcing? Consult STAND UP. What do you do if you're faced with a drowning, cardiac arrest, flat tyre or hangover? You'll find Three of the Best steps in SURVIVAL. Check out FUEL for the answer to a busy woman's plea: vegetarian and non-vegetarian meals you can make in less than 15 minutes. DOWNTIME is about good times, but also tackles getting out of our comfort zone and trying new experiences.

In our grandparents' day, books that were really valued were encyclopedic in their range. The famous *Pears Cyclopaedia* was on everyone's shelf; you could look up the best common cold relief and the capital of Mongolia, all in one easy volume. Then the World Wide Web blew the information age into everyone's home and encyclopedias looked rather quaint – anyone could put information into cyberspace. The problem is that everyone does, so there is lots of information and no quality control.

It's easy to understand how we can feel like we are not on top of our lives. There are so many demands on us as career women, parents and household administrators, as well as expectations that we should stay fit and look good. There's a lot of information out there, but we don't always have it to hand when we need it. So with one small book, providing straightforward options, we give you *Three of the Best*.

FIT

DISCLAIMER

Every effort has been made to ensure that the contents of this section are as accurate as possible. Neither the authors nor the publishers can accept responsibility for any injury suffered as a result of this material. Always consult your doctor about concerns arising from any exercise program and stop any physical activity that causes pain or distress.

JUMP-START GOOD HEALTH

You feel you haven't got time to get fit, firm up or lose weight? Do these Three of the Best for a month and you'll feel so good that you'll make time for more.

1. DRINK MORE

You need eight glasses or 2 litres a day, according to the US Institute of Medicine. Water is best but unsweetened fruit juice, in small amounts, and herbal tea count too. Keep a jug of water on your work desk and keep sipping. Take a water bottle in the car with you when you are doing the school pick-up. Add lemon for an extra detox kick.

2. MOVE MORE

Walk for 30 minutes every day. Walk to the shops instead of driving. Walk up and down the stairs instead of using the lift. Do some gardening on the weekend or get out of the office at lunchtime.

3. EAT MORE REAL FOOD

Most of the time, what you eat should look like it did when it was dug up, picked or caught – in other words, food that is in its natural state rather than processed. You can choose from vegetables, fruits, legumes and rice, lean meat, low-fat milk and eggs. Try a vegetable you have never eaten before.

DESIGNING YOUR TOTAL FITNESS: THE THREE FS

Here are Three of the Best elements for designing your own fitness program. Everyone exercises for slightly different reasons, but most women want a good level of cardiovascular fitness and a supple, well-toned body. The three Fs for feeling fabulous are: fit, firm and flexible. Write down the exercise you did last week. Does your list include the three elements of fit, firm and flexible?

1. FIT

It is vital that your program involves exercise where you huff and puff, or cardiovascular exercise. This might be walking, running, cycling, swimming, rowing, singles tennis, dancing, skating, netball or group classes like aerobics. We know that people who regularly exercise in this way are less likely to have chronic heart disease, high blood pressure, type 2 diabetes, high cholesterol and weight problems.

You need this sort of exercise three to four times a week at moderate intensity to be fitter than the person sitting next to you on the bus. Moderate intensity means that if '0' is sitting on the lounge watching a movie and '10' is the hardest exercise session you can think of, you'll be exercising at around '6'. If you can't have a conversation while you are exercising you are overdoing it. You'll need to have a go for about 30 to 60 minutes each session. If you are time-poor or very unfit you can break your sessions into 20-minute lots.

2. FIRM

Weight training is really good for women. You won't produce enough testosterone to end up with huge muscles but you will improve your posture, guard against osteoporosis and injury, and improve the strength and tone of your body. You'll also kick-start any weight loss you want to achieve and, of course, look gorgeous. As you travel through life from the end of school years to the age of your grandmother, you will lose 50 percent of your muscle mass. The good news is you can counter that with simple exercises (like those in the following pages) and it's never too late to start. Don't go to a gym if you don't want to; you can use some handweights (even tins of food) and your own body weight to great effect at home. Try to factor in a few home sessions a week by choosing two exercises for each body 'bit'. Leave your weights out on display in the room you spend most time in to remind you. If you do go to the gym, ask the instructor on duty to help you get acquainted with the equipment and to check out your style with handweights.

3. FLEXIBLE

Being supple means you will reduce muscle tension, avoid muscle injury and stiffness and help your stress levels. Try sitting on the floor with the soles of your feet against a wall. Gently bend from the hips over your straight legs towards your toes. Hold that stretch and if you can go a little further all the better. If you didn't make it to your toes then start reading 'Sitting hamstring stretch' (see 'Upper leg stretches' on page 34). In any event, incorporate stretching into your 'fit and firm' sessions by stretching before you exercise, while you exercise and after you exercise. It only takes a few minutes and you will feel wonderful.

FIRST STEPS TO EXERCISE

No matter what exercise you are up for, here's how to get ready.

1. THE DOCTOR

If you are over 55 years of age or haven't exercised for a long time, visit your GP before putting on your joggers. Your doctor will want to know if you have any history of high blood pressure, asthma, high cholesterol or cardio-pulmonary disease.

2. THE SHOES

Try to buy the best shoes you can afford for any sport that requires even the smallest amount of impact, including walking. Find a shop that sells service, not just sports equipment, so that the shoes can be fitted by someone who knows about footwear. Different types of sports shoes cater for different kinds of feet and different activities.

$3.$ THE ACCESSORIES

A cap, comfortable clothing, good-quality socks and a support sports bra are necessary parts of the total look. You will also need a factor 30+ sunscreen (water resistant if you're likely to sweat) and a water bottle.

Drink a glass of water 20 minutes before you start exercising and drink regularly as you go. It's also important to keep rehydrating after you exercise. If you feel thirsty and your urine is yellow then you are already dehydrated.

An optional accessory is a pedometer. Clip it onto your waistband and it will monitor how many steps you take each day. Most people average about 5000 steps; for fitness and good health your aim is 10 000. A pedometer will factor in any incidental activity, such as hanging out the washing, so you can feel better about housework! Another good toy is a heart-rate monitor, which records details about your exercise intensity and calorie burning.

VITAL EXERCISE COMPONENTS

Every time you exercise, whether it's to be fit or firm, your exercise program should have these three components:

1. WARM UP

Always do some light exercise to prepare your body and brain for your exercise session. It might be five minutes of gentle walking or cycling as a general warm-up before your power walking. If you are short on space, do some marching on the spot. If you plan to use handweights, try doing some of your exercises without the weights for five minutes.

After you have warmed up, do some stretching. Remember to stretch to tension but not pain.

2. WORK OUT

This is the main body of your exercise program, whether it's walking, running, cycling, swimming, team sport or working with handweights. You can always take a break during your session with some stretching, particularly if you are feeling overwhelmed. Remember to keep the water bottle handy. If you can't chat while you exercise then you are probably overdoing it, and for no real purpose.

3. COOL DOWN

After a work-out you need to let the body recover and gradually decrease your breathing rate, blood pressure and heart rate. Slow down with some gentle walking with deep breathing for five minutes. Once you have recovered, do some stretches. Try lying outstretched on the ground and reaching your feet and hands away from your trunk. Use some of the stretches suggested for specific muscle groups in the following pages.

3 FIRMING UP

When working with handweights or even using the resistance of your own body weight, here are three tips to make your work-out safe and effective.

1. BREATHING

When lifting handweights or using your body weight, such as in a triceps dip, always 'exhale on effort'. In other words, breathe out for the hard bit. So as you raise your upper body for an abdominal crunch (which is hard because you are going against gravity, and those stomach muscles would prefer to be lying flat in front of the TV), breathe out. As you lower your body you 'inhale on easy' and prepare for the next exhale.

2. POSTURE

First up, check your spine is in neutral alignment. It should be relaxed with your lower back in a natural slight curve. Your chin should be tucked down slightly so that you are looking at the horizon. As you start to lift the handweight, gently brace your stomach muscles and keep a level pelvis, which means don't tilt it backwards or forwards. Check to make sure your knees are in line with your toes. Most of us are round-shouldered from too much intimacy with the computer screen, so think about standing tall and relaxed.

3. JOINTS

Always keep your joints, where two or more bones meet, relaxed. You should never lock your elbows or knees when you are doing an exercise. So if you are lifting handweights, for example, in a biceps curl, your knees should be slightly bent or 'soft'.

STOMACH FIRMERS

To get a firm stomach there are two things you have to do: take off some of the belly fat and firm up the stomach muscles that are hiding underneath. Unfortunately, reducing the belly by just doing lots of abdominal exercise won't work because you can't spot-reduce fat. Instead you will need to combine some cardiovascular exercise and work on your six-pack with these Three of the Best exercises. The good news is that you only need three short sessions of these exercises each week to set yourself on the road to great abdominals.

1. THE ABDOMINAL CRUNCH

In the old days these were called sit-ups and the idea was to do lots of them with your legs flat to the ground. This is no longer considered a good idea, as people with sore lower backs will tell you. They are now called crunches, rather cruelly sounding like there might be a chocolate bar involved.

Try starting with 15. Concentrate on doing them slowly and well, then increase the number as you improve. Soon you will be able to do 15, take a short break and do another set of 15. Remember: if there is pain, refrain.

a. Lie on your back on a flat surface. Bend your knees with feet flat on the floor and cross your arms over your chest. (You can put your fingers behind your ears and elbows flat to the side if you want to make it harder, but don't yank your head up with your hands.) Breathe in.

b. Curl your spine up off the floor so that your forehead moves towards your thighs. Only lift your shoulders off the floor. This should take about three seconds. Breathe out as you go up and think about your stomach muscles. Relax your neck by imagining you have an orange cradled under your chin.

c. Return your spine to the floor while gently breathing in. This should take about two seconds.

2. THE OBLIQUE CRUNCH

This lovely exercise will strengthen and tone your side stomach muscles, also known as external obliques.

a. Lie on your back on a flat surface. Bend your knees with feet flat on the floor and cross your arms across your chest. Breathe in.

b. Curl your spine up as you would for an abdominal crunch but, as your thighs loom into view, gently turn your right shoulder to your left knee. Breathe out as you curl up.

c. Return your upper body gently to the floor, inhaling. Repeat with your left shoulder turning to your right knee, breathing out as you curl up.

d. The timing for the oblique crunch is the same as for the abdominal crunch; three seconds up and two seconds down. Don't rush it, enjoy it.

3. THE REVERSE CURL

The reverse curl is a strange little exercise because it doesn't feel or look like much is happening! It's very good for the lower half of your stomach (the upper half being flushed with the success of all those abdominal crunches you have done).

a. Lie on your back on a flat surface. Put your legs in the air as if you were resting your heels on a large fitness ball with your thighs at 90 degrees to your body.

b. Hold your legs in that position and put your arms, palms down, by your sides on the floor for stability. Breathe in.

c. Gently contract your stomach muscles so that your bottom becomes slightly airborne as you breathe out. Slowly lower to floor.

d. The movement is controlled; don't swing or rock your legs like a small marsupial in death throes. Make sure your lower back does not arch away from the floor by thinking about your navel pressing back to your spine. Start with 15.

UPPER ARM FIRMERS

Toned upper arms can be yours, whatever your age. The target muscles are the biceps brachii and the triceps brachii. The biceps is at the front of your upper arm; you see it quiver when you pick up that heavy bag of groceries or potting mix. The triceps brachii at the back of the upper arm may look like it is has gone on permanent holiday but don't worry: you can firm up and treat those tuckshop-arm jokes with the contempt that they deserve. Do these Three of the Best in the privacy of your own home if you like, aiming for three short sessions a week.

You may want to buy a set of handweights. They are inexpensive and will really kick-start your toned-arm regime. Test-drive them in the sports store to determine your starting weight, which will probably be around 2, 3 or 4 kilograms. Soon you will be able to do 15 to 20 of each exercise, take a short break and do another set.

1. THE BICEPS CURL

a. Stand with your feet shoulder-width apart. Holding one handweight in each hand with palms facing the front, inhale.

b. Keeping your upper arms still and close to your body, bend your arms at the elbows to bring your lower arms up towards your shoulders, palms up. Exhale as you go. It should take about three seconds to reach the top of the arc.

c. Slowly lower your forearms in a downward arc while you breathe in.

d. Try starting with 15 and remember to keep your body in a neutral posture. Don't swing your arms or sway your back. If you keep your abdominals braced you'll be working on your fabulous abs and protecting your back. It is better to lift a lighter weight, or no weight at all, and keep good form.

2. THE TRICEPS DIP

a. Find a stable chair, park bench or step and sit on the edge of your perch. Place your hands next to your thighs on the edge of the seat with your knuckles facing to the front and palms down.

b. Slowly lower your bottom off the seat towards the ground. Bend your arms at the elbow whilst keeping them close to the side of your body. Keep your body close to the seat edge and breathe in as you descend.

c. Lower until your upper arms are horizontal to the ground and then slowly return to your perch position. Breathe out as you go.

d. Try doing 12 dips. Don't be disheartened if you feel shaky. You are using a neglected muscle and taking the full weight of your body.

You should keep your body well balanced and look straight ahead. Your feet should be set out comfortably so that you form a chair shape with your body in the starting position. You can progress by moving your feet further away from your body line or balance on your heels rather than the flat of your feet when you feel stronger. Once you have mastered the technique and made some progress, be a total show-off by performing the exercise with one leg extended out to the front.

3. THE RECLINING TRICEPS EXTENSION

a. Lie on your back on the floor with knees bent and feet flat on the floor. Hold your handweights firmly above your chest with straight arms, palms facing each other.

b. Inhale and, keeping the handweights a head's width apart, lower them to your ears by bending from your elbows. Exhale while slowly taking the weights back to the starting position. The aim is to keep the upper part of your arms still so that you are making steady arcs from the elbow.

If you are wobbling then the weight is too heavy; to avoid skull trauma, try a lighter weight or, better still, practice without a weight first. Try starting with 15 extensions.

THIGH AND BOTTOM FIRMERS

This is the region where fat really likes to settle for retirement. Relying solely on dieting will probably make you feel disheartened because fat generally falls away from the upper body first and, unfortunately, you can't spot-reduce it from your bottom or thighs. Instead, take up some cardiovascular exercise to reduce unwanted fat generally, and target the muscles of your nether regions with three sessions a week of these Three of the Best firming exercises.

1. THE SQUAT

This exercise is great for the big muscles at the front of your legs (the quadriceps) and it also recruits the biggest muscle you own, the gluteus maximus, or bottom. It also works the hamstring muscles at the back of your legs. Once you have got the technique under your belt, hold your arms out in front to make it a little harder or use handweights by the side of your body. If you are finding it too demanding, find a wall or fence post and squat with your back against the support, so that the top half of your legs are parallel to the ground.

a. Stand with your feet hip-width apart and your knees 'soft'. Cross your arms across your chest so they don't flap in the breeze.

b. Slowly bend your knees and, at the same time, push out your bottom as if you were about to sit on a deep lounge. It's important that your chest is pushed forward slightly but not to the point where you can feel strain on the lower back. Take three seconds to get down to the 'deep lounge' position but not so far that your hips are lower than your knees or your knees extend over your toes. Breathe in as you go.

c. Slowly rise back to your starting position, breathing out.

2. THE SIDE LEG LIFT

This exercise will work your outer thigh. You can do your weekly quota lying on the floor watching TV. The slower you do it, the better.

a. Lie on a flat surface on your left side. Rest your head on the floor on your left arm and check that your body is in a straight line, with your left hip directly below your right hip and your right leg resting directly on your left leg. To keep yourself in a straight line, put your right palm on the floor for a bit of stability.

b. Slowly raise your right leg and then lower. Try 20 to begin. Don't take your right leg too high. Breathe in as the leg goes up and breathe out as the leg goes down.

c. Swap over to your right side and repeat the exercise.

While you're down there, you might as well get acquainted with your inner thighs. In the same starting position put your top leg onto the floor, bent at a right angle to your body. Gently and slowly lift the bottom leg up and down, keeping it just off the floor as it lowers. Don't forget to do both sides.

3. THE LUNGE

This exercise will work all the muscles of the upper leg and recruit your stomach to stop the wobbles. Try it outside for five minutes while you are doing your power walk.

a. Stand with your feet together in a nice, level position and put your hands on your hips. Bring one leg forward as if to take a step. Slowly bend your knees and release your back heel up as you lower your body. Your head, shoulders and hips are all dipping downwards in a straight line. Breathe in.

b. As you breathe out, return to the starting position. Repeat with your other foot leading the way, then keep alternating between right and left leading feet.

If you are finding it difficult stepping back and forth to the starting position, try leaving the front leg in position and go up and down like a carousel horse. Then swap and put the other leg in front.

Go slowly. In a good lunge your back knee will go close to the ground but, if you have a case of the wobbles, be more conservative. Try 12 to start. Once you have mastered the technique you can begin moving forward with travelling lunges on alternate legs or hold handweights by your side.

CORE MUSCLE STRENGTHENERS

By strengthening your core muscles (those clustered around your abdomen and spine) you will improve your posture, avoid back problems and increase your flexibility. Practise these three times a week, and don't forget to back them up with good posture when working at your desk.

1. THE HOVER

a.   Lie facedown on the floor, arms bent at the elbow, palms down. Now support yourself by taking your weight on your elbows, forearms and toes in a slightly elevated position.

b. Visualise your body as a soft piece of wood and hold that position with your eyes looking down at the ground. If you could see yourself in a mirror side-on you would be in a straight line.

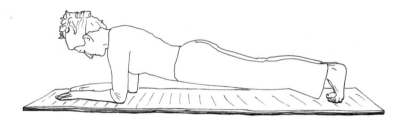

c. Breathe in and out in a controlled way and think about supporting your body weight by gently drawing in your muscles around your navel.

d. Hold the position for 30 seconds if you can, then gently lower your body to the ground. Sit back on your haunches with your arms stretched out in front of you to stretch. As you get stronger, extend your hovering time.

2. OPPOSING ARM AND LEG RAISES

a. Position yourself like a table with your hands, knees and shins on a flat surface. Don't sag your back. Make sure you are looking down to the ground so as not to strain your neck.

b. Slowly raise your right arm out in front of you. At the same time, extend your left leg straight out behind you. Both your arm and leg are parallel to the ground. Breathe out as you go.

c. Return your right arm and left leg to the table position. Breathe in. Repeat with the left arm and right leg. Do 10 or 20 on each side. If you want to make the exercise tougher you can raise light handweights as you go.

d. Go slowly to keep a 'stable table'. Your shoulders and pelvis should remain in a relaxed but steady position. Think about your abdominal muscles and brace them so as to control your movement. Imagine that a glass of your favourite drink is sitting between your shoulderblades and you don't want to spill a drop.

3. THE BRIDGE

a. Lie on your back on the floor with your knees bent, feet flat and slightly apart and arms by your side. Breathe in.

b. Raise your bottom gently off the ground to create a straight line from your shoulders to your hips to your knees. Don't push your hips up beyond the line of your body; this is not an arched bridge. Brace your stomach muscles. Breathe out.

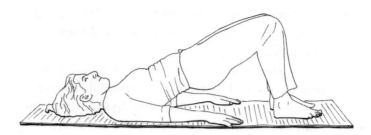

c. Hold the position for a moment and return your
    bottom gently to the floor. Breathe in. Try 15 to
    begin. When you have it under control, take one leg
    off the floor and hold it horizontal to the ground
    while still maintaining a good line with your body.

BACK STRENGTHENERS

Up to 80 percent of adults in Australia suffer from back
pain at one time or another. We are always lifting
something, whether it's children or shopping. Spending
20 minutes a few times a week on these Three of the
Best exercises will save you pain in the long run.

1. OPPOSITE ARM AND LEG LIFTS

a. Lie facedown on the floor with your arms straight out
    in front of you like a flying superwoman. Breathe in.

b. Slowly raise your right arm and your left leg while breathing out. Hold for a moment and then lower as you breathe in.

c. Slowly raise your left arm and your right leg while breathing out. Hold for a moment and then lower as you breathe in. Keep alternating between opposing arms and legs. Do 10 or 20 on each side to start.

2. SUPPORTED ROW

a. Find yourself a park bench or coffee table that is about the height of your knee. Stand side-on and rest your left knee and shin on the bench. Place your left palm on the bench.

b. Your right leg is now slightly bent and your right arm is by your side holding a handweight. Your eyes are looking ahead to the horizon. Breathe in.

c. As you breathe out, draw your right elbow up toward the line of your back. It will feel like you are pull-starting a lawnmower.

d. Slowly lower your arm back to the starting position while breathing in. Don't rush and you will feel the upper back responding. Do 20 and then swap sides.

3. LOWER BACK EXTENSION

a. Lie facedown on the floor with your arms by your sides. Breathe in.
b. Slowly raise the upper part of your body off the floor. Remain in contact with the floor from the hip bones down. Breathe out as you come up and only go as far as is comfortable.
c. Lower to your starting position as you breathe in. Repeat five times.

FITNESS IDEAS FOR A SPARE 5, 10 OR 30 MINUTES

1. *Five minutes.* Have a go at the pelvic floor exercises in 'Neglected but necessary exercises' on page 28 then practise them every time you have a spare five minutes during the day.
2. *Ten minutes.* Take on the push-up challenge in 'Neglected but necessary exercises' and work on your strength and style. If push-ups seem daunting, aim for strong abdominals instead with ten minutes worth of 'Stomach firmers' on page 11 every second day.

3. *Thirty minutes.* If you have a reasonable level of fitness, try working out for less time but harder. Power walk (no slower than 7 kilometres an hour) for about one minute then cut the pace for the next two minutes. If you're a runner, push yourself a little harder for one minute and jog for the next two minutes. Keep the pattern up for half an hour.

~

NEGLECTED BUT NECESSARY EXERCISES

As women we are very focused on upper arms, thighs and abdominals when we think about firming up muscles. Here are Three of the Best for the neglected but necessary bits: pelvic floor, chest and calf muscles.

Pelvic floor exercises are very obliging. You can do them anywhere and anytime. Do them when there are ads on TV or when you stop at a red light. A lack of muscle tone in this important region leads to stress incontinence and a reduction in sexual sensation. Need we say more? Start now, no matter what age you are.

Push-ups are a worthwhile challenge. Set aside two minutes a day to conquer the push-up; by the time you can do one well, you will be hooked. Once you can do five, include them at the end of your power walks. They look so impressive when aired to the general public.

Give your calf muscles a few minutes workout when you're stuck standing in the bus or check-out queue.

1. THE PELVIC FLOOR

a. Tighten the muscles in your lower pelvis by squeezing as if you wanted to stop yourself from urinating.
b. Hold the squeeze for as long as you can and relax for a few seconds before the next one. Eventually you will be able to do five squeezes in a row holding each one for ten seconds five times a day. Don't hold your breath while you're holding the squeeze but breathe rhythmically.

2. PUSH-UPS

There are three push-up positions depending on your upper-body strength. The box push-up with knees and forelegs on the floor, the half push-up or what was once described as the woman's push-up and the full push-up on your toes like Rocky. Start with the half push-up:

a. Support yourself on hands and knees, looking to the floor. Your hands should be a bit more than shoulder-width apart. Cross your feet at the ankles and raise your feet slightly off the floor, straightening your torso. It is important that your body is in a straight line from your head to your knees.

b. As you breathe in, lower your upper body down towards the floor by bending your elbows. Don't have your bottom high up in the air nor your back sagging like an old hammock.

c. Slowly bring your upper body back up to the starting position as you breathe out by straightening, but not locking, your elbows. It is better to do a couple well than lots badly, so if you have the shakes, regroup into an easier position.

3. CALF RAISES

a. Stand with your feet comfortably apart and hold onto a pole or doorframe for support.

b. With the right leg bent, take that leg slightly off the ground. With all your weight on the left leg slowly raise up onto the ball of your left leg. Pause and slowly lower back down. Try 15 and then swap legs.

Breathe rhythmically and don't rush. If you have the wobbles, perform the same move on both legs for greater support.

WAYS TO PROGRESS YOUR FIT PROGRAM

After a few weeks, your cardiovascular fit program
will become easier and now's a good time to move
to the next level. There are a number of ways you can
do this, but introduce the changes one at a time and
don't forget to still incorporate your warm-up,
cool-down and stretches.

1. FREQUENCY

Increase the frequency of your cardiovascuolar exercise.
If you are power walking four times a week, increase it
to five times. We know that very good fitness levels can
be maintained with three or four aerobic work-outs a
week but adding an extra session or two will bring an
even higher level of fitness.

2. INTENSITY

Increase the intensity of the session; so if you have been
enjoying three sessions of walking each week, you might
like to try jogging for one session or a combination of
walking and jogging in each session. Set yourself targets
within the session so that you jog for one block and walk
the next, for example.

3. VARIETY

Introduce some extra challenges into your work-out. If you have been walking, devise a new route with some hills or stairs. Introduce some skipping and step-ups into your routine.

Stepping up for the step up: Find a high step or low wall. Using alternate legs, put one foot up followed by the other foot. Make sure your feet are completely grounded on the step for stability; don't step onto the ball of your foot and let your heel hang. Step down and repeat as if you are marching. Try timing yourself for two minutes.

THIRTY-MINUTES FIT SESSIONS

1. Do 30 minutes of strengthening and firming without any equipment. Try push-ups ('Neglected but necessary exercises' on page 28), abdominal crunches ('Stomach firmers'on page 11), triceps dips ('Upperarm firmers'on page 15), the hover and opposing arm and leg raises ('Core muscle strengtheners'on page 22) and squats ('Thigh and bottom firmers'on page 19).

2. Try walking with extra zing – seek out hills and stairs and carry light handweights.

3. Go for a swim. Pick your favourite stroke and don't stop when you get tired: just use the kickboard for a while or do some shallow-end walking. Don't feel confident? Have a swimming lesson while you're at the pool.

SAFE STRETCHING

1.

Stretch to the point where you can feel the stretch in a strong way, with some tension, but not with pain. You should be breathing deeply and feel relaxed. If you are panting or not able to breathe rhythmically, you are overstretching.

2.

Hold the stretch for at least 20 seconds. As you do, feel the tension ease in the muscle and this will allow you to extend the stretch further if there is no pain. Never bounce while you stretch.

3.

Only stretch warm muscles, so go for a walk or march on the spot before you stretch. Stretch as part of your warm-up before you exercise, and stretch again as part of your cool-down after exercise. It's a good idea to stretch while you are exercising, so pause for a stretch while you are out walking or jogging or when the whistle blows for half-time.

UPPER LEG STRETCHES

Use these Three of the Best as part of your warm-up, workout and cool-down.

1. SITTING HAMSTRING STRETCH

a. Sit on the floor with your right leg out in front of you and your left leg bent so that the sole of your left foot is resting on your right inner thigh.

b. Slide both hands down your leg toward your right foot. You are bending from your hips, not the waist, so your back is straight and your eyes are on your right foot.

c. Hold for at least 20 seconds as you feel the tension in the back of your upper leg.

d. Swap legs and repeat the process. Don't forget to breathe rhythmically.

If you find it difficult to stretch your hamstring in the seated position because you are feeling the strain in your back instead of the back of your legs, try the standing up version.

a. Find a low seat or the low horizontal of a fence. Place your right heel straight out in front of you on the seat while supporting your weight on your left foot. Point the toes of your right foot up towards the sky.

b. Bend over from the hips to touch your right toes or the best you can do in that general direction. Hold for at least 20 seconds, feeling the tension along the back of your upper leg.

c. Swap legs and repeat the process. Don't have your leg up too high; 60 centimetres off the ground is good. Breathe rhythmically.

2. STANDING THIGH STRETCH

a. Stand with your feet together in a relaxed pose, holding onto the back of a stable chair or a rail.

b. Bend your lower right leg up behind you so that your right foot is below your right bottom cheek. Hold your right foot with your right hand so that you can maintain the position. Make sure your knees are close together.

c. Hold for at least 20 seconds, feeling the tension along the front of your upper leg.

d. Swap legs and repeat the process. Don't forget to breathe rhythmically.

If you find it difficult to stretch your quads standing up because of the wobbles, try the lying down version.

a. Lie on the ground on your right side with your left leg bent at the knee, resting your head on your arm on the ground.

b. Pull your left foot up under the left cheek of your bottom with your left hand. Hold the position for at least 20 seconds feeling the tension along the front of your left leg. Swap sides.

3. SITTING INNER THIGH STRETCH

a. Sit on the ground but, instead of crossing your legs, put the soles of your feet together so that your knees are high to the ground.

b. Gently push your knees down so they approach or, even better, touch the floor. If you like, use your hands to gently put downward pressure on the knees.

c. Hold the pose for at least 20 seconds and repeat. Breathe rhythmically. Don't bounce your legs. It's a gentle, controlled movement.

BACK STRETCHES

1. SEATED HUG

a. Sit on the floor with your legs crossed.

b. Place each hand on its opposite knee, curl over and pull gently.

c. Hold for at least 20 seconds, release and repeat several times. Breathe rhythmically.

2. SPINAL ROTATION STRETCH

a. Lie on your back on the floor with your arms out at right angles to your torso. Bend your right knee and twist it across your body so that it rests on the floor to the left-hand side. Use your left hand to push the knee towards the floor. (If your knee doesn't want to make contact with the floor, don't worry — you will improve with practice.)

b. Hold the position and if you are able, gently roll your head to the right, so you are looking away from your knee. Hold and breathe rhythmically for at least 20 seconds.

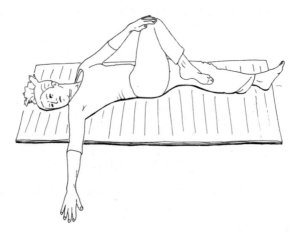

c. Return to the starting position and repeat with your left knee twisting over to the right-hand side.

3. CAT STRETCH

a. Begin on all fours with your knees about hip-width apart in a 'table' position, palms directly under your shoulders and elbows soft. Make sure your eyes are looking down to the ground.

b. Gently and slowly arch your back upwards like a cat stretching. Hold, breathe rhythmically and then relax to your starting position.

c. Gently and slowly relax your back until it sinks into the opposite position. Make sure your eyes are still looking at the ground. Hold, breathe rhythmically and then relax to your starting position.

UPPER BODY STRETCHES

1. CHEST STRETCH

a. Stand next to a tree trunk or in a doorway with your feet hip-width apart. Bend your left elbow up and sideways to 90 degrees and keep it at shoulder height.
b. Press the lower half of your left arm against the trunk or doorframe.
c. Step forward and feel the slight pressure as your chest opens up and your shoulderblades draw closer together. Hold for 20 seconds or longer but don't exert a lot of pressure. Breathe rhythmically.
d. Step back and release the arm. Repeat for the right side of your body. To increase this stretch further, gently rotate your body away from the stretching arm.

2. SHOULDER STRETCH

a. Stand with your feet hip-width apart. Hold your left arm out in front of you at shoulder height. With your right hand, hold the outside of the elbow of your left arm.

b.   Gently pull your left arm across your chest with your right hand. When you have gone as far as is comfortable, hold for at least 20 seconds. Breathe rhythmically.

c.   Release the left arm. Repeat with the right arm.

3. ROLLING UPPER BODY STRETCH

a.   Stand with your feet hip-width apart. Raise both your arms out in front of you at shoulder height and link your fingers.

b.   Turn your palms away from you and push out with your hands as your arms straighten.

c.   Your shoulders should gently roll in and you will feel the shoulderblades open up as you hold the position for at least 20 seconds. Breathe rhythmically.

60 MINUTE FIT SESSIONS

1.   Go to a new class: try fitball, spin, boxing, yoga or pilates.

2.   Play your child's favourite sport with them.

3.   Find your closest national park (www.australiannationalparks.com) and go for a bushwalk with a buddy.

WAYS TO STAY MOTIVATED

You've decided to get started on being 'Fit,
firm and flexible'. For the first two weeks you are on
fire, just looking at your exercise diary makes you
feel proud, and then all of a sudden you are
too busy. Here are Three of the Best to keep you
on track.

1. REASONS

Write down the reasons that propelled you into your
exercise program. It might be that you want to be able to
play with your children, or you want to go on a walking
holiday and not be the one always at the back of the
pack. Perhaps you want to feel confident in your bikini.
Keep the reasons in your exercise diary and read over
them often.

2. GOALS

Turn your reasons into goals by putting a due date on
them. Don't just say that you want to be thinner or
firmer: write down that you want to feel comfortable in
your old jeans or strapless dress in two months time.
Note the due date for your goal in your exercise diary
but make sure it's something achievable. If you are

aiming for weight loss then half to one kilogram a week is reasonable. If you are unrealistic in your goal setting and timescale you will just make yourself miserable. In fact the idea is to feel positive and focused.

3. PLAN FOR FUN

Make sure your exercise program is one that you look forward to. If you have always loathed going to fitness centres then get some handweights and enjoy your home gym. Write down all the physical activities you liked when you were younger or that you were good at as a schoolgirl, then draw up a weekly program with different kinds of activities that make you feel happy. Monday lunchtime for netball, Tuesday morning for power walking, Wednesday evening for weights at home, and so on. Alternate 'fit' days, when you do cardiovascular exercise, with 'firming' days, when you do strengthening exercise. Don't forget to factor in a day of total rest.

If you like company, find yourself an exercise buddy. Ask a friend of similar fitness and time constraints to come power walking with you twice a week or play singles tennis. If your friend loves aquarobics, try something new.

ASSESSMENTS FOR BODY FAT

You can do your own body-fat assessment with these Three of the Best methods. Simply standing on scales can be misleading as kilograms don't differentiate between lean muscle and fat. These methods will give you an accurate picture of where you are at so you can plan where you would like to be. It is also valid to put on your favourite pair of jeans and acknowledge that the waistband is now uncomfortably tight and perhaps the reason is not hot-wash shrinkage. On the other hand, if you work out that you are sitting in the 'healthy weight' range then stop worrying about those few kilos.

1. MEASURE YOUR WAIST

Fat above the hips carries a greater health risk than fat on or below the hips. There is a connection between chronic heart disease and the fat around your belly. Women should have a waist measurement of not more than 80 centimetres. If you are a Pacific Islander, it's 100 centimetres; if you are Asian, it's 80 centimetres.

2. BODY MASS INDEX (BMI)

Take your weight in kilograms and divide it by your height in metres squared. So if you weigh 70 kilograms and you are 1.5 metres tall, your BMI is: $70 \div (1.5 \times 1.5) = 31$.

Once you have your 'number', consult the World Health Organization table:

<18.5	Underweight
18.5–24.9	Healthy weight (low health risk)
25–29.9	Overweight (moderate health risk)
30–39.9	Obese (high health risk)
>40	Morbidly obese (very high health risk)

3. WAIST TO HIP RATIO (WHR)

WHR is a method used to measure body fat above and below the waist. Measure your waist (at the navel line) and divide that number by your hip measurement (at the widest point). Women with a WHR of greater than 0.8 are at more health risk than those below 0.8.

EXERCISE FOR FAT LOSS

If you have done your Three of the Best 'Assessments for body fat' (see page 43) and decided that you need to lose weight, here are the exercise tips that will get you on your way.

1. WHAT

Choose some cardiovascular exercise that you really enjoy, such as jogging, walking, rowing, swimming or cycling. Try a combination of these sorts of exercise to keep you motivated. In between exercising, keep moving as incidental activity – such as changing the channel without the remote, or bypassing the dryer to hang out the washing – also helps weight loss.

2. HOW AND WHEN

Do your exercise sessions at a low to moderate intensity. That means on a scale of 0 to 10 (where 0 is watching the midday movie and 10 is the hardest session you can think of), you should be aiming for around 3 to 5. If you are fit or have a long history of exercise, go for a 5+ rating. Aim for 60 minutes a session; you can break your session into three lots of 20 minutes if you have to, but weight loss is enhanced if your session is continuous. Aim for exercising every day and keep a record of what you have achieved in your exercise diary.

3. WITH

Along with your shiny new exercise plan, cut back on saturated fat in your diet. Try to minimise hot chips and other fried foods, pies, quiches, pastries, biscuits, fatty meats, coconut and palm oil and butter.

DESK STRETCHES

1. THE CHIN TUCK

a. Sit in a relaxed position and look straight ahead.
b. Move your chin back gently as if to make a double chin. Keep your eyes looking forward.
c. Hold the position for five seconds then relax. Repeat five times.

2. SEATED SPINE STRETCH

a. Sit in a low-back chair, plant your feet firmly on the floor and cross your arms across your chest.
b. Gently lean back over the top of the chair as far as is comfortable and enjoy the stretch for five seconds before returning to the upright position. Repeat five times.
c. While you are in the starting position, turn your head, upper body and shoulders to the right as far as you can comfortably go. Hold for five seconds then repeat for the left side. Repeat five times.

3. HAND AND ARM STRETCH

a. Stretch out your right arm in front of you, palm facing down.

b. With your left hand, gently pull back the fingers of your right hand towards your shoulder. Hold the stretch for five seconds and relax. Repeat five times. Do the same stretch on the left hand and arm.

DESK HEALTH

It doesn't matter whether you work from home or in a commercial office, your life at the desk can be vastly improved by these Three of the Best.

1. THE SET UP

If you are distracted by the lure of the kitchen's biscuit tin, set up a fruit bowl on your desk. Have a piece of fruit before you get the 4pm munchies so you are not tempted by less healthy options. Also, set yourself up with good posture from top to toe. Your eyes should be level with the top of your screen, which is directly in front of you, and your shoulders should be relaxed. Your elbows should be at 90 degrees when your hands are resting on the keyboard. Is your seat adjustable and supportive to ensure that your hips and knees are also at 90 degrees? Make sure your feet are flat on the floor or footrest.

2. THE ROUTINE

Every 30 minutes you need to get out of your chair and give your eyes a rest from the computer screen. Try Three of the Best 'Desk stretches' (page 46), or fill up your water jug, or just breathe deeply while you look out the window.

3. THE BREAK

Don't forget to have lunch away from your desk. No matter how busy you are, always eat something healthy away from your workstation, chew slowly and then give yourself some digestion time. It's a good idea to get outside. If you are not too far up in the sky, take the stairs instead of the lift. Get together with some workmates and walk for 30 minutes.

FITNESS INCIDENTALS

1. Do a shop at the greengrocer without the car. You'll get fit and firming exercise as well as tonight's dinner.
2. Walk your children to school or home and get exercise with all the news.
3. Ring up a friend who lives 6 kilometres away and meet her halfway on foot for a morning cuppa.

ENERGY AND EXERCISE

1.

You can get your energy from fats and protein but if you asked your muscles, they would tell you that carbohydrates are best. If you cut out a lot of the good (complex) carbohydrates as some diets suggest in an attempt to lose weight, you'll just feel tired and that means less exercise and less weight loss. It is much better to give your body the fuel it needs so you can throw yourself into your 'Fit, firm and flexible' exercise program.

2.

Your daily diet should be made up of at least 40 percent complex carbohydrates, which include grain foods like bread, breakfast cereals and pasta, as well as vegetables, legumes, fruits and nuts. Simple carbohydrates, or sugars, are fine in small amounts, but the trouble is that we don't generally eat small amounts: each week most Australians eat about 1 kilogram of sugar. Most of this is hidden in food that you may not even think of as 'sweet', such as savoury crackers.

3.

Your body can get all the sugar it needs from carb-endowed foods, and while you are eating those you get lots of other nutrients, which makes them very good value. If you are feeling flat in the afternoon and don't know how you will cope with that after-work aerobics class, an unsweetened fruit juice will get you going, or take a walk to a juice bar. We've been sold sugar-heavy energy drinks as a way to cram more into our busy lives, but these are probably only useful if you are running a half-marathon.

CALCIUM AND EXERCISE

1.

All through a woman's life, calcium is very important, specifically for your nerves, muscles, blood and, vitally, bone health. When your body is not getting enough calcium from food, it draws it from your bones. If that keeps happening you end up as a candidate for osteoporosis, a thinning of the bones. Bone density loss can occur during pregnancy, breastfeeding and menopause, the latter explaining why mature women are more at risk of hip fractures. Indeed, one in two women will sustain a fracture due to osteoporosis in their lifetime.

2.

We all need to build strong, dense bones by eating foods high in calcium such as milk, calcium-enriched soy milk, cheese, yoghurt, ricotta cheese, almonds, baked beans, canned fish with edible bones and broccoli. You need three to four serves a day (about 800 to 1000 milligrams), more if you are over the age of 70. If you can't get enough from natural sources, talk to your pharmacist about taking a supplement.

3.

Some factors that impact on our likelihood of developing osteoporosis are beyond our control, such as family history. Excessive alcohol and smoking don't help either. Exercise is really crucial to preventing and even reversing osteoporosis. It is never too late to start weight-bearing exercise like walking and some weight training. Osteoporosis Australia has an excellent guide for exercise and fracture prevention, as well as advice on diet, at www.osteoporosis.org.au or call 1800 242 141.

IRON AND EXERCISE

1.

If you are feeling too tired to exercise, you are in good company. You could be doing too much for family, friends or work — or you could be short on iron, which is the most common nutritional deficiency in women (about 8 per cent of us suffer from it). As a result of menstruation, growth, dieting and pregnancy, your haemoglobin becomes low and affects the delivery of oxygen to the cells in your body.

2.

A blood test by your doctor can tell you if you are anaemic, but you may already know the symptoms: more than acceptable tiredness and irritability, pale skin, brittle nails, feeling cold and a poor attention span. As most of this reads like a standard Wednesday afternoon at 4.15pm, it's a good idea to have the blood test if you're concerned.

3.

You need 12 to 16 milligrams of iron a day (less if you are over 50), which is obtainable from lean red meats, liver, kidney, seafood, chicken and, to a lesser extent, wholemeal bread, cereals, leafy green vegetables, legumes and baked beans. Tea and coffee lessen the absorption of iron while vitamin C improves it, so an orange juice with your breakfast cereal is a good start. All things considered, sometimes a supplement from your pharmacist is necessary.

ALCOHOL

1.

Women are more affected by alcohol than men because of our smaller liver and body weight, so keeping up with the other half of your touch footy team is not a game you will win. You should have no more than one to two drinks a day. A standard drink is:

- one middie of full-strength beer
- two middies of light beer
- one cocktail glass
- one shot of spirits
- 100 millilitres (two-thirds of a glass) of table wine.

Drinking 'in moderation' may mean drinking even less than that for you, especially when driving a car.

2.

Accumulating your daily allowance for a big night on the weekend is not only cheating but dangerous. Binge drinking (four drinks lined up over two hours) is very bad for you. How bad is bad? Too much alcohol contributes to weight gain, heart and liver disease, high blood pressure, stomach and menstrual problems, insomnia, headaches and some cancers. Not to mention doing those silly things and having no memory of it the next day.

3.

Start your bar tab with a large glass of mineral or soda water (drop in a slice of lime and you'll feel completely sociable). If you need half your daily allowance to loosen up when you get to the bar, then drink some water before you leave home. After your first drink, have another water 'chaser'. Quench your thirst from the salty bar snacks with water, not alcohol.

BEAUTIFUL

SLOWING SKIN AGEING

There are two main factors in how quickly our skin ages:
our genes, an internal factor, which we can't do
much about, and external influences, such as smoking,
sun exposure and hard living, which we can do
something about.

1. DON'T SMOKE

We know the damage it can do to our long-term health,
but smoking also accelerates the ageing process so that
most smokers appear ten years older than their
biological age. The sobering truth is that for smokers,
middle age starts in their thirties. The skin loses its glow
and lines start to appear, particularly around the
mouth. And that's just the beginning; eventually it leads
to the dreaded Smoker's Face, with lines radiating from
the lips, numerous shallow lines on the cheeks and
lower jaw, deep lines around the eyes, and a loss of tone
and elasticity that exceeds the normal ageing process.
Then there's the possibility of terrible gum disease.

There are numerous ways to stop smoking. Cold
turkey works for many, but dealing with the withdrawal

symptoms may be too difficult for the heavily addicted. 'Nicotine fading' involves gradually decreasing the nicotine content of cigarettes smoked over a few weeks, starting with 30 percent less nicotine in the first week, 60 percent in the second, and 90 percent in the third. But don't compensate by taking more puffs or smoking more cigarettes.

As nicotine is the addictive but not the harmful component of cigarettes, it can be substituted in the form of patches, gums, inhalers and lozenges, and this can work well, particularly if combined with some form of behaviour modification. There is often a ritualistic aspect to smoking, so replacing one ritual with another can help, for instance the morning cuppa with a cigarette could be replaced with a walk.

There are also prescription medicines available, which should be discussed with a GP. These work by reducing the pleasure derived from smoking and help lessen withdrawal symptoms. But there can be side effects, such as nausea, headaches, insomnia, disturbed dreams and changes in food tastes. Some prescription drugs have also been linked to depression and even suicidal thoughts. Doctors obviously need to be careful about who they prescribe these drugs to; they may not be suitable for anyone with a history of depression. A study at the University of Helsinki in Finland found that persistent smokers are more prone to depression than non-smokers, and that depression is likely to increase in the initial stages when they stop smoking but will eventually decrease if they succeed in staying away from cigarettes. Many smokers who suffer from depression are able to quit if treated with antidepressants and behavioural therapy.

Hypnosis is another possibility, and acupuncture is sometimes used but seems to be less successful. Laser therapy, advocated by some clinics, where a low-level laser is pointed at various acupuncture points, is expensive and of extremely dubious value.

2. SUNSCREEN

The best thing you can do for your skin is to use sunscreen. Exposure to sunlight causes 90 percent of the symptoms of premature skin ageing. Ultraviolet radiation from sunlight causes wrinkles by breaking down collagen, creating free radicals and inhibiting the natural repair mechanisms of the skin. You can see its effects by comparing skin on face, neck and arms with skin on less exposed areas.

But it's important to use sunscreen correctly. Sunscreen should be applied liberally enough to all sun-exposed areas to form a film when first applied. It takes ten minutes or more to be absorbed by the skin so it's a good idea to apply it after a morning shower and then hang around in your undies or a bathrobe before dressing to avoid contact with clothes, particularly shirt collars. Apply sunscreen after moisturisers and body lotions, but it's okay to apply it under liquid make-up, which in itself offers some protection. Sunscreen can irritate the eyes, so avoid the eye area; wearing sunglasses and some make-up takes care of that.

If you are indoors most of the day one application should be enough, but sunscreen should be reapplied after two hours of exposure to the sun. It should also be reapplied after swimming or excessive sweating. Insect repellents reduce a sunscreen's sun protection factor (SPF) by as much as a third, so when used in conjunction a high SPF sunscreen should be used and reapplied more often.

Choose a broad-spectrum cream (one that blocks UVA and UVB radiation) and has an SPF of at least 15. Read the label and ensure the ingredients titanium dioxide, avobenzone or zinc oxide are included. Some older formulations remained on the surface of the skin and looked unattractive, but newer formulations containing micronised or microfine titanium dioxide absorb well and are just as effective. An oil-free base is best for everyday use.

> **Note** that a small amount of exposure to the sun is desirable as it provides vitamin D to your body which, among other things, helps us absorb calcium, so it's okay to leave it off, say, your arms when you're not going to be outside for longer than half an hour. But always wear it on your face and neck.

3. ADOPT A MODERATE LIFESTYLE

Living hard and knocking ourselves about shows in our faces. Admittedly, there are exceptions — Marianne Faithfull, for one, and a few supermodels. But while the rest of us might get away with it in our twenties, after that it's time for a healthier lifestyle. That means getting a good night's sleep, doing some exercise, keeping weight under control, drinking about eight glasses of water a day, and having a moderate (at most) intake of alcohol. You only have to look in the mirror after a night on the tiles to see the way alcohol piles on the years. As we age it takes longer to get back to normal, and there can be permanent effects such as broken veins.

Long-term excessive alcohol consumption can, of course, damage the liver and heart and, because it interferes with the body's ability to absorb calcium, can lead to osteoporosis. The good news is that a little red wine is good for us, increasing our resistance to heart disease. During a ten-year study by the *American Journal of Medicine*, researchers discovered middle-aged teetotallers who started drinking alcohol have a 38 percent lower risk of developing heart or artery disease than those who avoid it. Those who drank only wine had an even lower risk. But bear in mind that even moderate drinking has been linked to breast cancer.

CLEANSING, TONING AND MOISTURISING

1. CLEANSING

It's important to do this every morning to keep the pores clean, particularly around the nose area. If you use a cream cleanser, apply before stepping into the shower. The steam will help it do its work. If you use a foaming type cleanser, apply in the shower. At night, nothing divides off the working day better than taking off make-up. Even if you're going out again, it's nice to make a fresh start. Cold cream type cleansers and oils do a better job of removing make-up than foaming cleansers. Smooth on the cleanser and tissue off, then apply another lot and tissue off again. Use a warm face washer to finish the job. Even if you don't wear make-up your pores can become clogged so you still need to use a cleanser, which can be any type you feel suits your skin. Apply, tissue off, then finish with a warm face washer. There are many excellent, well-priced cleansers available in supermarkets.

2. TONING

Toners are widely believed to close the pores, but this is debatable. There is, however, a skin-tightening effect that makes this seem the case, and they leave the skin feeling refreshed and invigorated. Choice of toner depends on skin type. If your skin is dry or normal, avoid toners containing alcohol – these are only for oily skin as they are drying. Even if you have excessively oily skin, don't try to compensate with frequent applications of alcohol-based toner because this can lead to excess oil production as the skin tries to compensate for moisture loss.

If you wear make-up, toning at night is an important step to complete the cleansing process because make-up can be hard to shift. It also helps to remove oil-based or cream cleansers. You may have to use a few cotton balls soaked with toner before the skin is completely clean.

You can make your own toner. If you have dry or normal skin, use rosewater (available at pharmacies) on its own, or mix 50 millilitres of rosewater with half a teaspoon of alum (also available at pharmacies) and 100 millilitres of glycerine, then bottle and store in the fridge. For oily skin, use witch-hazel (which also works well on a soothing eye-pad for a lie down) or mix one teaspoon of alcohol (from the pharmacy not the bottle shop!), 100 millilitres of distilled water and half a teaspoon of alum, then bottle and store in the fridge.

3. MOISTURISING

It doesn't prevent or eliminate wrinkles, but moisturiser temporarily makes them look better by keeping the skin moist and reducing the appearance of fine lines. Dry skin in itself doesn't cause wrinkles – the reasons are more complicated, due partly to genetic factors, gravity, and also the damage we do to ourselves, with sun exposure and smoking the leading causes. But dry skin certainly makes wrinkles look worse.

While a moisturiser isn't a substitute for sunscreen, a sunscreen is a good addition to moisturisers and doesn't affect the texture or feel on the skin. The things to remember are to apply liberally, and don't rely on it alone during prolonged exposure to the sun — it's fine, though, for a day in the office with limited exposure. *Choice* tested 26 daytime moisturisers containing sunscreen and the following emerged as the top three: L'Oréal Paris Visible Results Daily Skin Perfecting Moisturiser SPF15 ($26.95, 50 ml), Dove Essential Nutrients Protective Day Cream SPF15 (the cheapest buy at $8.60, 50 ml), and Garnier Nutritionist Regenerating Daily Moisturiser SPF15 ($15.60, 50 ml). The testing included products ranging in price up to $175, further proof that expensive isn't necessarily best when it comes to skin care.

Night creams are as essential to dry or normal skin as the cream we apply in the morning. As we sleep, our bodies repair themselves and that goes for skin as well. The enzymes that help renew our skin need moisture to function properly. Night creams are richer and heavier than day creams — how heavy and rich depends on how dry or oily your skin is. Before applying, your face and neck should be thoroughly cleansed and toned. Allow plenty of time before you actually rest your head on the pillow as most night creams take time to soak in. Night cream can be alternated every few days with a pierced capsule of natural vitamin E — give this plenty of time to soak in.

If your skin is very oily, use a day cream at night and sometimes leave it off altogether. And if you come home late and plan to go straight to bed, a day cream that will soak in quickly is fine.

As night creams are generally fairly heavy, it's best not to use them in the delicate eye area where the skin is thin and should be treated with care. Eye creams are light and absorb easily. Some come in the form of gel and have a nice, cooling effect. If you use a lotion-type moisturiser during the day, it can be used around the eyes as long as there are no warnings about this on the label. Cosmetic companies often claim that eye creams reduce puffiness and/or shadows under the eyes, but these claims are dubious. Puffiness and shadows are often caused by late nights and too much alcohol, although dark shadows sometimes run in families, so there is a limit to what an eye cream can achieve. But they feel nice and are generally opthalmologically and dermatologically approved, so they don't contain substances that are best avoided in the eye area. Eye cream should be applied with minimum pressure using the pad of the ring finger starting at the outer corner of the eye and moving in a figure of eight around both eyes a couple of times.

BEFORE, DURING AND AFTER SHOWERING

1. SKIN CLEANSING

It's important to cleanse skin in the morning as well as at night. If you have dry or normal skin and use a deep cleansing cream or milky cleanser, apply before you step into the shower. Leave it on and let the steam help it penetrate, then wipe off with a warm face washer before you get out. If you use a foaming cleanser, apply it while in the shower and wash off before you step out.

2. EXFOLIATING

Using a facial scrub is one of the more important things you can do for your skin and should be done once a week. It helps rid the skin of the dead cells on the surface, improving skin tone. But don't go overboard and exfoliate every day – the epidermis (the top layer of skin) is a protective barrier and dead cells can be a temporary part of the protection.

There are numerous cheap and effective facial and body scrubs on the market or you can make your own. For instance, a tablespoonful of brown sugar can be rubbed gently onto the face during showering, or equal parts baking soda and water is good for oily skin and loosening blackheads, while some oatmeal or cornmeal and a little water are good facial scrubs for dry skin. If skin is particularly sensitive, a rough face washer can serve the purpose.

It's worth doing arms, legs and any other exposed parts of the body as well every few weeks, and this is where home preparations come into their own as they are so cheap. An old-fashioned loofah or an exfoliating glove is useful too.

3. BODY LOTION

After a shower, body lotion counters the drying effects of water and soap on skin, particularly if the water is fairly hot. There are many good body lotions on sale in supermarkets; sorbolene is excellent – and cheap. It's only worth going upmarket if you want a particular scented lotion. In fact, cheap versions in the categories of cleansing, exfoliating and body lotions can work just as well as expensive ones.

MAKE-UP TIPS

1. CONCEALER

This comes in different forms with a limited colour range; aim for a colour similar to your skin tone. A crayon – keep it sharp – is good for the inner corner of the eye where most of us have a deep purple shadow. A wand applicator with a creamy concealer is good under the eyes. Most make-up experts recommend applying concealer under foundation, but for amateurs like us that tends to smear and dilute the effect, so try applying it over foundation and see how that works for you.

2. EYES

Apply foundation to eyelids first, then powder, so that you have a good base that will help make-up last all day. Don't feel you have to match eyeshadow to eye colour – in fact, a reddish brown shadow can make blue eyes look bluer. Make-up expert Sonia Kashuk, author of *Real Beauty*, recommends using hair colour as your guide, so blonds look good with creams and light taupes, brunettes with mochas and chocolate browns, and redheads with coppers, peaches and reddish browns. Grey hair is good with grey, lavender and soft blues.

Unless it's a special occasion when you're going for a super-glamorous look, don't go for multi-colours. A wash of one-colour cream eyeshadow over the eyelid gives a soft, natural look.

Use an eyeliner pencil, if you like. Liquid eyeliners are much harder to wear, so if you do the line should be very thin, or even dotted and smudged a little. Go for a mascara that doesn't contain those little lash-building hairs, which can create an unnatural, clumpy look.

3. THE SUNLIGHT EFFECT

In summer, less is definitely more. Keep colours close to your natural colouring (think roses, browns and beige) and consider a tinted moisturiser or sunscreen instead of foundation. Take a mirror (preferably magnifying) into the sunlight to check make-up.

MAKE-UP MISTAKES TO AVOID

1.

Don't outline your lips in liner darker than your lipstick. It looks artificial and accentuates fine lines around the mouth.

2.

Don't contour with darker shades of face powder and foundation. Trying to sculpt cheekbones by applying brown powder to the hollow underneath never works. Much better to apply a little blusher to the cheekbone, making it more pronounced.

3.

Always allow moisturiser to absorb before applying foundation, and allow foundation to settle before applying powder. Apply moisturiser after showering and wait ten minutes of so before starting on your make-up. When applying make-up, leave face powder until the end except for the eyelids, where it's a good base for eye shadow.

MAKE-UP OVER FORTY

Forty is the new thirty, and fifty is the new forty, etcetera. But sometime in the forties, signs of ageing start to appear and need to be taken into account with your make-up and fashion choices.

1.

Skin tends to dry as we age, so the first step is moisturiser massaged into the skin for maximum benefit. On the lower part of the face, foundation should be used more as a concealer than complete cover. Blend it in so that it isn't obvious. Save concealer for the dark spot near where the eye meets the bridge of the nose and dab a little on dark shadows under the eyes after applying foundation. Check for any 'cracking' after 15 minutes.

2.

A magnifying make-up mirror — or, even better, a magnifying make-up mirror with a built-in light — is one of the best aids to facing the world with confidence about your look.

3.

As a general rule, 'shimmer' and very dark colours are best avoided on the face and also the nails, once skin starts to age. Keep eye shadows fairly light and neutral — shades of taupe work well, and greys and soft mauves can work particularly well with silvery or grey hair. If you use eyeliner, pencil gives a softer effect, but if you prefer a liquid, avoid black and go for a slightly smudged effect, particularly beneath the eyes.

AU NATUREL LOOKS

We don't always have a lot of time for applying make-up, and some of us prefer to go without much of the time anyway. If spending time outdoors, apply sunscreen to your face, avoiding the eye area – you'll need sunglasses for that. Make-up gives some protection from sun damage, so sunscreen is particularly important when not wearing any. But there are other minimal steps we can take to look good (almost) naturally.

1.

Dab a little foundation in the dark inner corners of our eyes and on any dark shadows – an amazing improvement in seconds.

2.

If your lips are naturally pale, apply a lip crayon in a slightly darker shade to the natural pigment all over, then add a coat of lip balm.

3.

Use a tinted moisturiser to give the overall boost of a little colour.

FIVE-MINUTE MAKE-UP

1.

Apply foundation, blending carefully at the hairline and neck. Powder the eyelids, then apply eye shadow — a lightish taupe colour suits most of us. Apply mascara then brush eyebrows using a pencil to touch-up if needed .

2.

Use a concealer to lighten the inner-eye corner, and powder any shiny areas such as the nose and chin.

3.

If you use blush, dust a little along the cheekbone, then apply lipstick or lip gloss.

THINGS YOU NEED TO KNOW ABOUT COSMETIC COMPANIES

1.

The links between cosmetic companies may surprise you. More than 75 percent of cosmetic lines are owned by Estée Lauder or L'Oréal. Estée Lauder owns Aramis, Aveda, Clinique, Bobby Brown, Prescriptives, MAC, La Mer and Donna Karan Cosmetics, as well as the cheaper brands now sold through Target — American Beauty, FLIRT! and Good Skin; L'Oréal owns Maybelline, Lancôme, Helena Rubinstein, Biomedic, Vichy, Biotherm, Giorgio Armani Parfums, Ralph Lauren Parfums, Redken and Garnier; Procter & Gamble owns CoverGirl, Max Factor, Clairol, Olay, Pantene and Vidal Sassoon; Revlon owns Almay and Ultima II; Beiersdorf owns La Prairie, Nivea and Juvena; and Johnson & Johnson owns Neutrogena, Retin-A and Renova. Bear this in mind when choosing between a cheaper brand and one of the more expensive lines, as the costly research that goes into developing products is usually undertaken by the umbrella company and shared among their offshoots. The quality of ingredients is the same and products have been developed by some of the best brains in the beauty business. It's all about different styles of marketing and targeting different markets.

2.

Treat every claim made by a cosmetic company with a high degree of scepticism. Advertisements make claims about 'miracle' ingredients with unsubstantiated benefits, and these claims don't come in for the rigorous consumer scrutiny that would apply to almost any other product.

3.

Cosmetic ingredients are listed in order of concentration, so water often heads the list: at the end of a long list, ingredients will be present in very small amounts.

COSMETIC GIVEAWAYS

Cosmetic companies selling some of the more expensive brands promote them with giveaways. You can get a good deal by waiting until 'free gift' time to buy an expensive cosmetic (this is obviously not usually high demand times such as Christmas and Mother's Day). The gifts provide an opportunity to try new products, including skin care, make-up and perfume, often presented in very attractive toiletry bags. Free make-ups are often part of the deal and can be worthwhile for ideas and a new look. But these are definitely hard-sell sales opportunities, so be strong!

1. TOP END

Estée Lauder was one of the first to make a regular feature of gifts with purchase, and its sister company Clinique followed on. Clarins also has regular gift offers, which usually involve buying two products including one skin care item. As these are expensive lines, it's important to genuinely want the purchase and not just buy it to take advantage of an offer. Three products worth trying at offer time are Clinique Dramatically Different Moisturising Lotion, Estée Lauder Advanced Night Repair Protective Recovery Complex and Clarins Beauty Flash Balm, which seems to give a bit of a glow to skin when applied before make-up.

2. MID-RANGE

Revlon and Elizabeth Arden often have attractive gift offers with moderate expenditure. Revlon Age Defying Make-up is an oil-free foundation that gives nice, light coverage. Elizabeth Arden Ceramide Defining Skin Brighteners, a moisturiser, and Revlon Vitamin C Absolutes Overnight Renewal Cream are worth a try.

3. BUDGET

Avon also has worthwhile gifts with purchase, such as buy one product and get another free, or several at a bargain price.

LIPSTICKS

A big breakthrough in cosmetics has been the development of lipsticks that last all through the day – or night – surviving eating (as long as the food isn't greasy), drinking and even kissing! The formula was developed by Procter & Gamble, owner of Max Factor and CoverGirl, and they were the first to launch these lipsticks that truly match up to the claims made for them. Maybelline has since come up with its version.

They are applied in two stages: colour first then, after a minute or two, the top coat, which is a clear layer that's similar to a balm and gives lips gloss. The colour layer must be applied carefully as mistakes are difficult to remove (if necessary use an oily make-up remover). Ensure your lips are clean and dry before applying the colour sparingly, then smooth it out with a fingertip and leave it to dry, which takes at least a minute. Then apply the top coat; this will need to be touched-up during the day, but you don't need a mirror to do it. Because it is used more frequently, the second coat tends to run out first, but you can substitute with a lip balm. The Max Factor top coat is also now sold separately and can, of course, be used with the other brands.

Summing up, Max Factor and CoverGirl are ahead on staying power, so if you can find colours you like, go for those brands. But Maybelline is a pretty good alternative. Prices are a guide only.

1.

Max Factor Lipfinity ($29.95; Moisturizing Topcoat sold separately, $15.95).

2.

CoverGirl Outlast ($22.95). Widely available in department stores, pharmacies and some Coles supermarkets.

3.

Maybelline SuperStay Lipcolor comes in a nifty pack with colour one end and clear coat the other ($17.95). It's not quite as stayfast as the other two.

GREAT HAIR

1. ADDING VOLUME TO MEDIUM-LENGTH AND LONG HAIR

Wash hair and towel dry, then hang your head forward and brush and blow-dry your hair. When dry, use velcro rollers to create the style you want. Leave the rollers in for five or ten minutes, remove and brush into shape. It's not necessary to use any styling products and if blow-drying is one of your talents you don't need to use this method. You can give your hair a lift even when not washing it by putting it in velcro rollers before you step into the shower and removing them after.

2. STRAIGHTENING HAIR

If you have no one to help you, blow-dry hair then divide it up by rolling it onto velcro rollers. Heat your straightening iron and then, removing one roller at a time, use the iron to straighten hair, curl by curl.

3. AVOID USING PRODUCT OTHER THAN SHAMPOO AND CONDITIONER

Mousses, gels and other styling products are expensive, contribute little except in the hands of professionals, and tend to make hair washing a daily chore.

EYEBROW SHAPING

1.

The most important thing to remember about eyebrows is that once plucked hairs may not grow back. Fashions come and go, but it's important to think of the long-term and go for a look you can live with for the rest of your life.

2.

Pluck stray hairs from underneath the eyebrows, never on top. And don't be tempted to pluck inwards further than level with the inner corner of the eye. The outer end should extend slightly beyond the outer corner of the eye.

3.

If you have gone too far in the past or lost eyebrows for any other reasons, Avon Glimmerstick Brow Definer is an excellent eyebrow pencil that gives a soft, natural result. Maybelline Expert Eyes Brow and Liner Pencil has a built-in sharpener and a dry texture that stays put if you want a firmer line. Often a good result can be achieved by filling in gaps in eyebrows using a powder eyeshadow in a taupe colour or another brownish shade. Or you can resort to cosmetic tattooing (see page 113).

MANICURES

Manicures, like a lot of other beauty treatments, are turning into girls' nights out. A Melbourne group organises 'Makeovers, Manicures and Martinis' nights in clubs; for $50 you get a mini makeover, a mini massage and a mini manicure plus a martini. An ordinary salon manicure will set you back about $30 but, indulgence factor aside, it's easy to achieve a good result at home. Be prepared to allow at least an hour; read or listen to music as the paint dries. A good home manicure can last up to two weeks. Here are the three steps.

1. PREPARATION

First apply a rich hand cream, rubbing it into the cuticles, and let it soak in. Then decide what shape you want. A lot depends on what you do with your hands; if it involves housework, young children and cooking, an oval shape that doesn't extend beyond the tips of the fingers is best. Otherwise it depends on fashion. But avoid short, square nails as they can make hands look chubby and unattractive. Use an emery board to shape, using the rougher side first and the other side for fine-tuning and buffing out any ridges on the surface of the nails. Using nail scissors first to achieve a rough shape can save time, but an emery board for final shaping is essential for a good result. Line up your hands and check that the nails on both match.

2. PAINTING

Even if your nails are unpolished, you need to wipe them with nail polish remover to dissolve any oils left on the surface from the hand cream. Then apply a base coat; this might seem unnecessary, but it will help the polish to adhere and also keep the nails from discolouring if coloured polish is used constantly. Choosing a colour is a matter of personal preference, fashion and, in the case of a special occasion, the outfit you'll be wearing. If hands aren't your best feature, a paler shade is best and avoid glitter and fluorescents. Apply two thin coats of colour, allowing ten minutes drying time in between. After 15 minutes, apply a clear top coat or another layer of the base coat for extra protection. If you want a quick result that looks natural, only better, just apply a base coat. It gives a slight gloss without the artificial shine of a clear polish.

3. PROTECTION

It's essential to allow 45 minutes for drying before doing anything that could smudge the nails. Even going to bed can result in sheet marks on the nails when you wake up. Nails may be touch dry, but once more than one coat of polish is applied, ample drying time is needed. When you are sure the nail polish is completely dry, give your hands a good massage with hand lotion.

NAIL FIX-ITS

1. If you smudge polish during a manicure, dip the pad of a finger (not the nail!) from the other hand in nail-polish remover and use it to smooth out the smudge. Apply another coat of polish or top coat.

2. If fingers are stained from nicotine or nails are stained from the constant application of nail polish, try rubbing in some whitening toothpaste or lemon juice. It's a good idea to give nails a break from nail polish every few weeks to restore shine to nails. When nails are polish-free, rub in a little vitamin E oil every night.

3. When a nail breaks it's usually best to trim it off, but minor repairs can sometimes be made by cutting a tiny strip of gauze from a teabag, laying it over the break and painting over.

PEDICURES

At about $35, having the occasional salon pedicure is one of life's little luxuries (many salons offer a double deal of pedicure and manicure for $50). But it can be a relaxing experience to give yourself a pedicure at home too.

1.

You will need a basin big enough to hold both feet (like an old-fashioned washing-up bowl) and have a nice, fluffy towel on stand-by. Remove any old nail polish. Pour in enough warm water to cover your feet and throw in some bath salts. Soak feet for five minutes or so, then use an exfoliating scrub or wet pumice stone to smooth out any rough patches of dry skin. Dry one foot and use an orange stick to push back the cuticles. Repeat with the other foot. Rub in some soothing cream; peppermint cooling lotions are excellent. Rest your feet on the towel until the lotion is absorbed.

2.

Use nail clippers to cut the nails straight across. Length is up to you, but it must be below the end of the toe and allow room for regrowth before the next pedicure. Use an emery board to finish, aiming for a square shape with slightly rounded corners. Buff nails with the smoother side to even out any ridges. If your toenails are discoloured, try rubbing in some whitening toothpaste or lemon juice, let it dry and rinse off.

3.

Use nail-polish remover to clean off any lotion remaining on toenails. Use toe separators (which you can buy at pharmacies) or cotton wool balls (in which case, keep them clear of polish) to prevent toes rubbing together. Apply base coat, allowing five minutes for it to dry. Then apply two thin coats of colour, allowing ten minutes in between for drying. Colour does not necessarily have to match fingernails – you might prefer a darker shade on toes. Finish with a top coat or another application of base coat. Allow 45 minutes for drying but, if you can't sit down for that long, wear sandals that don't touch the toenails, or those crazy paper shoes they give you to wear if you have a pedicure while staying in a fancy hotel. A pedicure should last at least two weeks. A lot depends on what kind of shoes you wear – trainers can be hard on nail polish.

MOUTHWASHES

There's no need to buy a mouthwash. Not only are they expensive but many contain alcohol, a harsh ingredient which the *Journal of the American Dental Association* claims can actually make periodontal disease worse and provide a mouth environment that encourages the bacteria that cause bad breath. Here are three gentler versions that you can easily make at home.

1.

Baking soda (sodium bicarbonate) makes an excellent mouthwash — use about half a teaspoon in a quarter of a cup of warm water. You can also use baking soda to brush your teeth instead of toothpaste.

2.

A mixture of nine parts water to one part 6 percent hydrogen peroxide is effective at banishing bad breath. Use a tongue scraper (available at pharmacies) first.

3.

Half a glass of warm water with a teaspoon of salt stirred in makes a soothing gargle for a sore throat.

HOMEMADE FACE MASKS

Applying a face mask then lying down for 15 minutes
is a great way to relax while doing your skin some
good. Soak cotton balls in witch-hazel or toner to
cover your eyes or use rounds of cucumber. Never
use a face mask on the delicate area around the eyes.
There are many commercially available face masks
but if you use them, make sure you buy one that is
right for your skin type. But you don't need to go
further than your own kitchen to find the ingredients
to make your own. Try avocados, strawberries (as
long as you're not allergic), yoghurt, sour cream … it's
even possible to make a clay mask (good for oily skin)
using the clay kind of kitty litter – mix with a little
water, strain out the grit then use the liquid!

1.

Mash one ripe banana with a tablespoon of honey, a
teaspoon of lemon juice, a tablespoon of oatmeal, an
egg yolk, and a teaspoon of vitamin E oil (or use
wheatgerm oil) until it forms a smooth paste. Apply to
the face and neck, avoiding the eye area, and rest for
ten to fifteen minutes. Your skin will feel fresh and
relaxed.

2.

Eggwhite frothed up with a fork or whisk can be used on its own as a face mask. It will leave your skin feeling toned and tightened.

3.

If you have oily skin, try milk of magnesia (available at pharmacies). Smooth it on then rest while it dries and sets. Rinse with lukewarm water. It absorbs oil brilliantly.

HAIR REMOVAL

HOME

1.

Shaving is the most popular method for legs and underarms and the cheapest. It does not change the texture or rate of growth of hair; the regrowth just feels coarse because the ends are flat. There are two main types of razors: electric, designed to be used on dry skin, and blade razors, for shaving wet skin after a soapy lather. When using a blade razor, your skin should never be cold as goosepimples can lead to cuts, so, as the skin needs to be wet anyway, it's a good idea to shave in the shower or a warm bath. Use a shaving cream or gel, which will soften the hair, and keep wetting the razor while shaving. Change your razor regularly and never shave with a blunt razor. For legs, start above the ankle and shave upwards, taking extra care over the shinbone. Don't press hard and take your time. After drying, apply a soothing body lotion. If you have any razor nicks, dab on a mild antiseptic or use an antiseptic cream.

2.

Depilatories make hair dissolve so it can be wiped away. This chemical hair removal is effective, cheap and easy to use. Choose the type of depilatory to suit the purpose: depilatories come in different strengths and in the form of creams, foams or lotions. Read the instructions carefully and do a patch test first leaving on a small area of skin for ten minutes before washing off then waiting 24 hours in case any irritation results. Never use around the eyes – on eyebrows, for instance – as depilatories can severely damage eyes. Depilatories work well on the bikini line, which is not really suitable for shaving, and on legs. They are also effective in removing female chin and above-lip hair. When using any depilatory, apply and leave on the skin according to instructions then wash off with warm water. Dry skin and apply a soothing body lotion.

3.

Epilators are an effective but painful method of hair removal. These hand-held electric devices pluck hair out by the roots, but the process is more painful than tweezing or waxing; rotating metal spirals twist a bunch of hairs together before plucking them out, so it's not for anyone with a low pain threshold. Any form of plucking can result in some hairs not growing back, and because hair is plucked out by the roots, regrowth is slower than with shaving.

Home waxing is not as effective as epilators, according to a *Choice* survey. With waxing, hot or cold wax is applied and a strip of cloth is placed over the top. The cloth is then ripped off, taking hair with it. Cold wax is the least effective of all methods. Diabetics should not wax because of the greater risk of infections, and wax should not be used over moles.

> **Note:** No form of hair removal should be used if skin is sunburnt or irritated.

PROFESSIONAL

1.

Waxing is still the most popular form of professional hair removal. If this is your preferred method, it is more effective done in a salon than at home. Wax is heated then applied with a spatula in the direction of hair growth (downwards). A strip of cloth is placed over the wax, then the skin is held taut with one hand while the other hand rips the cloth strip off backwards, against the direction of hair growth. Ouch! It works well if done professionally, but more regrowth than might be desirable is necessary before it can be done again. A soothing lotion or gel should be applied afterwards.

2.

Laser hair removal is an increasingly popular but expensive form of hair removal. The upside is that some people achieve permanent loss of most (but not all) unwanted hair, but generally only after several treatments. Laser hair removal only affects hairs that are in the active growth phase at the time of treatment and not all hair follicles are at this stage at the same time. Most people need four to six treatments to achieve a satisfactory result. Because the laser targets many hairs at once, large areas can be treated in one session, with treatments taking anything from ten minutes to an hour. Laser energy is absorbed by the pigment (melanin) in the hair and transmitted down the shaft to the root, which kills the hair and makes it fall out. Light-coloured, grey or red hair cannot be removed by laser. It works best on light-skinned people with dark hair. Shaving the area a few days before will increase effectiveness. Treatment is less painful than waxing or electrolysis but is not completely free of discomfort. The application of a topical anaesthetic cream beforehand can help. Costs vary enormously so it's worth checking around, and it's important to check the credentials of the operator. Word of mouth is a good indicator.

3.

Electrolysis is the only method that can claim to remove hair permanently, although hormonal changes can cause new growth. But it is a slow process that is only suitable for small areas, such as women's unwanted facial hair. Each hair is treated individually by inserting a fine needle into the hair follicle and applying an electric current to destroy the hair root. The hair is then removed with tweezers. Only 30 to 40 hairs can be treated in one session. It's important to consult a properly trained operator; training is part of the Advanced Association of Beauty Therapists diploma course. The cost is usually about $25 for a 15-minute session, but even tackling a very small area such as above the lips can involve many sessions.

TEETH WHITENERS

HOME

1.

Use an electric toothbrush to achieve the feel of a professional clean. Electric toothbrushes make an amazing difference and many come with timers, which means that you really do brush for a full two minutes. Use a soft brush attachment and don't apply too much pressure, particularly around the gum line where it can cause receding gums leading to sensitivity, as below the gum line teeth don't have enamel coating. Let the toothbrush do the work; simply move it over the teeth and gums.

2.

Use a whitening toothpaste. Any of the cheaper brands sold in supermarkets will do as well as more expensive lines. You can also buy bands containing peroxide to place over the teeth, or simply dab some 3 or 6 percent hydrogen peroxide on a cotton ball and run it over the teeth – do this every morning.

3.

Don't smoke and avoid coffee and tea as they will stain your teeth. Red wine and food with strong colours, such as cherries and blueberries, can also stain. If you can't clean your teeth soon after eating or drinking, rinse your mouth with water.

PROFESSIONAL

Whitening teeth is one of the easiest ways to improve your appearance. Here are three of the best ways your dentist can help.

1.

The most popular method is a combination of dental surgery and home treatment. Your dentist takes an impression of your teeth and makes a custom-fitted flexible tray, which you fill with a whitening gel and wear for up to two hours daily or at night for about two weeks. Most whitening kits prescribed by dentists contain a solution of 10 to 15 percent carbamide peroxide, a very effective bleaching agent. Once you have the tray (or trays) you can order more gel and use again as necessary. Cost is $400 to $500.

2.

For a quick result you can have tooth whitening in the dentist's surgery. This involves coating the teeth with a paste of carbamide peroxide, then applying a light beam to the paste. Because the paste is much stronger than the whitening gel you use at home, the dentist 'fences off' the gum area to protect it. The procedure usually takes one-and-a-half to two hours and there is no follow-up. The results are equivalent to a dentist-supervised home treatment, but it is more expensive (about $1000).

3.

When it comes to the back teeth, old mercury-based silver amalgam fillings are a thing of the past, except in the case of large restorations. Nowadays dentists use a composite resin that can be matched to the colour of the teeth. Because the filling takes longer, the cost is one-and-a-half to twice the cost of amalgam fillings, but the lifespan is seven to ten years, similar to amalgam. In the past, this sort of tooth-coloured filling was only used on front teeth for cosmetic reasons because the old porcelain fillings lacked the staying power of amalgam and modern composite resins.

In some cases, the pre-fluoride generation are now experiencing a noticeable extension in translucency at the tips of upper front teeth due to wear on the biting edge.

This can sometimes be corrected by the application of a small amount of bonding to the back of the teeth that makes this translucency look opaque again. (Cost is about $110 a tooth.)

SOURCES OF BEAUTY FROM WITHIN

1. HAPPINESS

Being in love gives a special glow — as does good sex. But feeling contented and at peace shows in the face too. At times of unhappiness and stress, our faces reflect our anxiety. It's not always possible to avoid these situations, so it's important to learn to calm down and give ourselves a break. This might involve meditating (see *Peace*), or taking a walk while listening to some music. Going to a cheering movie or reading an engrossing book takes us out of ourselves too, creating some space from our problems.

If unhappiness is caused by grief it helps to express your emotions, talk to friends, and cry a lot — somehow crying makes us feel better, for a while anyway. Having a circle of good friends and keeping in touch is one of the best aids to happiness. Our spirits lift when we talk on the phone to a friend; even more so when we see them.

And it's a fact that giving to others and doing good makes us feel happy. The US National Academy of

Sciences monitored the brain activity of people choosing from a list of charities to which they would like to donate. As they selected a charity, the part of the brain dealing with joy was activated. Other tests conducted at the University of California found links between volunteering and longevity. In terms of happiness, it is truly better to give than to receive.

2. HEALTH

When we feel good, we look good. So it's important to have a balanced diet, exercise, get plenty of sleep, drink plenty of water and keep your weight under control. Smoking takes a toll on looks, ageing our skin more than any other factor except for long hours of unprotected sun exposure. Over-indulging in alcohol shows in our faces too: a look in the mirror is a shock for anyone suffering a hangover. So the message is to keep as healthy as possible and outer radiance will follow.

3. CONFIDENCE

Looking good has a lot to do with believing we look good, and that comes from confidence. Many of us are naturally shy, but taking an interest in others is a good way of disguising the fact. Being aware of what is going on around us helps to build confidence. Read newspapers, watch television news and current affairs, and listen to the radio. Keep up-to-date with movies and books.

Good grooming has a lot to do with confidence too. That means well-cut hair, nice hands, clothes that suit the situation, and make-up if you feel you need it — although it's good to feel confident enough to go without it sometimes. How we look is a factor in how others view us. Not that we have to always wear the latest fads, but be aware of trends and try to keep up-to-date, even if it only involves tying a scarf in a new way. It's not so much a question of looking fashionable as of not looking unfashionable. Reading a fashion magazine and wandering through a department store gives a feeling for the mood of the times. We have to feel good about ourselves before we can convince others.

COSMECEUTICALS

Cosmeceuticals is the new buzzword in skin care; it describes products that are a cross between cosmetics and pharmaceuticals. Many cosmetic manufacturers make extravagant claims for their products, boasting of magic ingredients that produce amazing results. But don't expect any miracles. There are two products that do have proven benefits: tretinoin and alpha hydroxy acids (AHAs). Also giving good results are fillers that are injected into facial lines to plump and smooth them out, as well as into lips, to make them more luscious.

1.

Tretinoin (retinoic acid), available in Australia in the prescription-only products Retin-A and Retrieve, is recommended by dermatologists for helping to remedy the symptoms of sun damage. It helps the skin to renew itself more quickly and improves the appearance and texture of skin by reducing the appearance of fine wrinkles, surface roughness and mottled skin discolouration. Used correctly, it gives the best result of any anti-ageing cream or gel. And at around $40 a tube, which lasts four to six months, it's a lot more reasonably priced than most.

The acid form of vitamin A, tretinoin works by increasing cell turnover, helping your skin shed dead skin cells and stimulating collagen production, which helps fight wrinkles. Melanocytes, the skin cells responsible for skin pigment, are suppressed by tretinoin. It takes about six months of use before you can expect to see maximum benefits. After six months a maintenance program is required; if treatment is discontinued, the benefits will fade.

Tretinoin cannot reverse severe skin damage. It's important to consult your dermatologist to find out whether it's suitable for you, then use it strictly as directed. Usually tretinoin is applied in a thin layer every second or third night, avoiding the lips and around the eye area, increasing to every night as tolerated. It's important that tretinoin is used as part of a skin care regime that includes moisturising and sun protection.

Tretinoin makes skin more susceptible to sun damage, so always use sunscreen and avoid prolonged exposure to the sun, particularly in the middle of the day. When using tretinoin, avoid any other product that can cause skin irritation, such as perfume and toners containing alcohol, on the face and neck.

Do not use tretinoin skin products without talking to your doctor if you are pregnant, planning to be, or breastfeeding. Peeling and skin redness are common side effects, but this transient skin irritation usually reverses quickly as your skin becomes accustomed to the treatment. If prolonged irritation, blistering or peeling occur, consult your doctor immediately.

Tretinoin is also used as an acne treatment, in which case expect acne to get worse in the first seven to ten days, but to improve after two to six weeks.

Tretinoin is available online, but it's not a product that should be used without the advice of a doctor. Over-the-counter products containing retinol, another form of vitamin A, are milder and less irritating to the skin, but not as effective. They are lower in concentration than formulations used in the clinical trials that showed measurable benefits.

2.

Alpha hydroxy acids (AHAs) have been used as a beauty treatment for centuries. When Cleopatra bathed in milk, her complexion reaped the benefits of its lactic acid content. Women in ancient Rome used the sludge from wine barrels in face masks and their complexions improved as a result of its tartaric acid content. In the 1990s, AHAs were rediscovered and incorporated into hundreds of skin rejuvenation products. Most cosmetic companies now have at least one AHA-derived product.

There are two different ways in which AHAs are commonly used. High-strength AHAs are included in chemical peels by dermatologists and there is convincing evidence that such peels can reverse some of the signs of skin-ageing. There are also home-peeling kits, but these contain AHA concentrations of 10 percent or less and research suggests such a low concentration is unlikely to be of much benefit. But home-peel kits are nevertheless cheap, convenient exfoliating agents that could be worth a try. Falling in-between in terms of effectiveness are peels available from trained cosmeticians, starting at a cost of about $80.

The pH (acidity) level of products containing AHAs is also important. In 1997 the Cosmetic Ingredient Review Panel (a US cosmetic industry self-regulatory body) concluded that AHAs are safe in consumer products for home use when:

- the AHA concentration is 10 percent or less
- the final product has a pH of 3.5 or greater (lower numbers indicate greater acidity)
- the final product is formulated to protect skin from increased sun sensitivity or its package directions tell consumers to use sunscreen.

AHAs are also used in low concentrations in a wide range of night and day creams, body lotions, face masks and hand creams. Of course, the concentrations need to be low for products designed to stay on the face all day or overnight, or even for the ten minutes a face mask normally stays on the skin. The higher concentrations used in peels are left on the skin for a few minutes, then washed off.

The main types of alpha hydroxy acids found in skin care products and their sources are: glycolic acid (sugar cane), lactic acid (milk), malic acid (apples and pears), citric acid (oranges and lemons) and tartaric acid (grapes).

AHAs act as a powerful exfoliating agent by encouraging the shedding of old surface skin cells. As we age, there is a gradual slowdown in the rate at which old cells are replaced by newer cells. Speeding up the process gives a fresher, healthier look with more even tone and texture. AHAs also cleanse and unblock pores and can be used in the treatment of excessively oily skin and acne. (In treatment of acne, however, beta hydroxy acid (BHA, or salicylic acid) is more commonly used as, unlike AHAs, BHA has the ability to penetrate into the pores, which makes it more effective in dealing with blemishes.)

Salon mini peels using AHAs in concentrations of 20 to 30 percent can be done by trained cosmetologists. Chemical peels using higher concentrations must be performed by dermatologists. Concentrations of ingredients aren't usually listed on packaging of home-peel kits, but you can always ring the company and ask.

Chemical peels can help correct mild sun damage, reduce light scarring, improve skin discolouration (age spots), iron out some fine lines and remove blackheads. Chemical peels cannot reduce the appearance of blood vessels on the skin or remove keloid (raised) type scars.

The two major side effects of AHAs are skin irritation (redness, burning, itching) and an increase of 50 percent in sun sensitivity (it's an odd paradox that products which help repair sun damage also increase sensitivity to UV radiation). Always use a broad-spectrum sunscreen with an SPF of at least 15 when using AHAs, but then that's sound advice at any time.

Anyone with darker coloured skin – and that even means olive-skinned people who tan easily and don't suffer sunburn – should use AHAs with caution because of the risk of pigment darkening.

Don't be seduced by skin care products based on AHAs with a high price tag. Alpha hydroxy acids are simple, inexpensive chemicals. Effectiveness comes down to the concentration and, provided that is the same, a cheap brand is as good as an expensive label.

3.

Australians of all ages, including women – and men – in their twenties and beyond, have taken to injectable fillers and Botox in a big way. According to an article in the *Courier Mail*, gatherings where like-minded friends get together with a doctor in attendance and receive injections in the name of beauty are a new spin on Tupperware parties. In spite of procedures costing about $350 a pop and having a limited life, more than half a million minimally invasive cosmetic procedures are performed in Australia every year, and the figure is rising.

People with plumper faces often look younger because they have fewer wrinkles; the problem is the plumper bodies that usually go with them. Injectable fillers work by plumping up the area being treated and therefore smoothing it out, a procedure known as soft-tissue augmentation. The main target areas are the nasolabial folds (between nose and lips), puppet or marionette lines (between the mouth corner and the jawline), crow's-feet, frown lines, fine lines around the lips, and the lips themselves for a more luscious look.

Hyaluronic acid is the most commonly used filler, but there are others; besides synthetic materials, doctors can use your own body fat if you choose. Most injectable fillers have a short life, from three months to a year; your body basically absorbs the filler. Aquamid is a permanent, non-biodegradable filler made from a sterile polyacrylamide gel; the cost of this treatment starts around $1200. Permanent fillers have a higher incidence of long-standing side effects such as allergies, lumpiness, infection and discharge, all of which can be difficult to manage. Doctors advise patients to try a more temporary treatment first to test the result. Two of the most commonly used hyaluronic acid treatments in Australia are Restylane and Juvéderm. These do not cause allergies and the results can last nine months to a year. The cost of treatment with these temporary dermal fillers starts at about $350.

Soft-tissue augmentation should only be performed by qualified professionals, that is, dermatologists and cosmetic and plastic surgeons. It is a quick procedure, but there is some pain, swelling, redness and sometimes bruising.

Botox is in a different category in that it works to paralyse the muscles that create facial lines. The effect only lasts for about three months, but when the muscles that cause us to frown, for instance, are given a rest, the result in terms of wrinkle reduction can be more permanent (provided we don't start frowning again). The Therapeutic Goods Administration (the Australian drug regulatory agency) approved Botox for cosmetic use in 2002, specifically for treating vertical frown lines. Botox is only available on prescription from a doctor and should always be injected by a trained medical professional who is familiar with the correct technique.

The downside of Botox is the frozen look that can result. In spite of its popularity in Hollywood, many directors hate it because it stops the face from expressing a subtle range of emotions. Other people's reaction to us depends a lot on the way our faces express emotion, particularly when we smile. If our eyes don't crinkle, others will see us as insincere. As for frown lines, how about a fringe?

THINGS YOU NEED TO KNOW ABOUT DOCTORS DEALING WITH COSMETIC PROCEDURES

1.

Plastic surgeons are trained through the Royal Australasian College of Surgeons (RACS). It takes a minimum of eight years after graduating as a doctor to qualify as a plastic surgeon. The RACS is recognised by the Australian Medical Council, and only plastic surgeon members of the RACS are affiliated with the Australian Society of Plastic Surgeons. You can check whether a doctor is a fully trained plastic surgeon by ringing the society's hotline on 1300 367 446 or visiting the website (www.plasticsurgery.org.au).

2.

The Australian College of Cosmetic Surgery (ACCS) has two faculties: the Faculty of Surgery and the Faculty of Medicine. Members of the surgical faculty have three years basic surgical training and then two years of specific cosmetic surgery training. Members of the medical faculty are not certified to perform invasive surgery such as facelifts and tummy tucks but they can do Botox injections, laser work and liposuction. The ACCS was formed in 1999 and has not been recognised by the Australian Medical Council. Members can be found on the website (www.accs.org.au).

3.

The Australasian College of Dermatologists (ACD) offers training and accreditation for members. After graduating as a doctor, dermatologists train for a minimum of two years in a teaching hospital followed by five years of advanced specialist clinical training. The ACD is recognised by the Australian Medical Council. There is a geographical register of dermatologists on the website (www.dermcoll.asn.au).

SKIN RESURFACING TREATMENTS

Chemical peels, dermabrasion and laser skin resurfacing are three procedures designed to refresh the appearance of the skin, and all achieve the same result using slightly different methods. A chemical peel exfoliates the outer layers of skin, while dermabrasion involves a technique similar to sandpapering the outer layers of skin. Laser skin resurfacing vaporates the outer layers of skin. These treatments are not an alternative to a facelift (which is an anti-gravity operation), but are sometimes used in conjunction. They improve the texture and quality of the skin, and may also improve the colour and lustre. There is a slight chance of complications such as altered pigmentation and scarring if the treatment is too deep, so ensure you have a qualified person looking after you.

1.

For a chemical peel, a solution which exfoliates layers of skin is applied. The peels vary from a lunchtime peel, which can barely be noticed apart from some mild flushing, to much deeper peels requiring days or even two weeks recovery time, with the possibility that some redness may persist for even longer.

2.

For dermabrasion, a high-speed rotating device is used under local or general anaesthesia. The wire brush (or diamond abrasion sander) removes layers of skin and leaves the skin bloody and raw after treatment. It may take a couple of weeks to return to normal activities and redness may persist for longer. Lasers have largely replaced dermabrasion as a safer and more precise skin resurfacing tool.

Microdermabrasion is a much milder form of treatment that is well tolerated and can produce short-term improvement in complexion. It works by spraying a jet of fine microcrystals across the skin, lifting dead skin cells which are removed by vacuum suction.

3.

Laser skin resurfacing is another alternative. Performed using a beam of laser energy which vaporises layers of skin, the advantage is that the level of penetration can be precisely controlled and there is little, if any, bleeding. Healing should be complete in seven to ten days depending on the depth, but redness will last anywhere from one to six months. The recent introduction of fractional lasers where microcolumns of laser beam are delivered into the skin have significantly reduced the downtime and side effects associated with resurfacing lasers. A milder form of treatment involves a broader bandwidth of light (IPL) that send light pulses into the skin layers (epidermis and dermis) while leaving the epidermis intact. IPL does not ablate or vaporise skin but selectively targets specific colours, such as red and brown, and is useful for treating broken capillaries and sun freckles and pigments.

Length of recovery following (and often results of) these procedures is largely dependent on the depth of treatment. These procedures involve some risk and should not carried out by anyone other than a plastic surgeon, cosmetic surgeon or dermatologist. Many of these procedures have to be used with caution in individuals with darker skin, starting from olive, as they can cause post-treatment pigmentation problems. As they make the skin more sun sensitive, it is important to wear sunscreen outside at all times.

ACNE

Acne is one of the most common headaches teenagers face. It is more frequently seen in oily skins and more boys than girls suffer from it. The causes are changing hormone levels and genetic factors. Adults can have acne as well, either ongoing from teenage years or seeming to come from nowhere at any age, often due to hormonal changes.

1. SEEK HELP EARLY

This is important to prevent scarring, and it's best to consult a dermatologist. There are many factors to consider including age, skin type, cause, severity and the types of lesions present, and there are many different treatment options. A dermatologist will consider all these factors and can also prescribe medication in higher concentrations than any sold over the counter. One option for severe cases of cystic acne is the prescription-only drug isotretinoin (Oratane or Roaccutane). It has a high success rate, but takes four to eight months to work. If a female patient is sexually active, the contraceptive pill or other forms of contraception must be used as well because of the danger of severe birth defects if conception occurs during treatment or in the month after treatment ceases.

2. BENZOYL PEROXIDE

A randomised trial conducted by Professor Hywel Williams and colleagues from the universities of Nottingham and Leeds in the UK, published in *The Lancet*, found that the anti-bacterial benzoyl peroxide is as valuable as prescription antibiotics in the treatment of mild to moderate facial acne. The trial, involving 650 participants, found most improvement occurred in the first six weeks of treatment. Benzoyl peroxide is marketed under a variety of brand names in over 200 formulations.

Three of the best known here are Oxy 5, a 5 per cent concentration (about $12 for 20g); Oxy 10, a 10 per cent concentration (about $16 for 25g); and Clearasil Ultra, a 5 per cent concentration (about $13 for 20g).

3. BETA HYDROXY ACIDS (BHAS)

In the form of salicylic acid, BHAs have been used in the treatment of acne for decades. BHAs are exfoliating agents that can penetrate oil-filled pores and break down the dead cells that clog pores and cause the inflammation that leads to pimples. Salicylic acid is a derivative of aspirin and has anti-inflammatory qualities as well (so it is not to be used by anyone allergic to aspirin). BHAs are present in many skin products.

> **Notes:** A combination of the above two treatments, benzoyl peroxide and salicylic acid, is often used; benzoyl peroxide kills the bacteria that cause pimples and salicylic acid reduces oiliness and unblocks skin pores, helping to reduce blackheads and whiteheads.

Acne scarring is difficult to correct; prevention is best. However the recent introduction of fractional lasers have advanced the effectiveness of laser scar repair. Whilst 100 percent correction is not possible, 50 to 70 percent improvement can be achieved after three to five sessions.

COSMETIC TATTOOS

If you don't feel comfortable without make-up, cosmetic tattooing is an increasingly popular way of being ready to face anyone whose path you may cross first thing in the morning. Cosmetic tattoos use different inks to those employed in traditional tattoo art. The colours are softer and more subtle, like the effect achieved with a colour pencil, and they are not designed to last a lifetime. Most fade gradually and disappear after five years. Bet some owners of ill-considered tattoos wish they'd gone for the cosmetic option! The good thing about the more temporary nature of cosmetic tattooing is that make-up fashions change, and you don't want to be stuck with one look forever. Also, as we age, less tends to be more in the make-up department. Here are the three most popular types of cosmetic tattoo.

1. EYEBROWS

We've all seen pictures of screen goddesses from the 1930s with their pencil–thin eyebrows. Since then, the fashion for thin eyebrows has come and gone again several times, and to varying degrees. The bad news is that eyebrows often don't grow back after drastic plucking, and even if you've plucked judiciously there can be gaps in the brow line that need to be filled in. If eyebrows have all but disappeared, colour can be implanted for a solid look or hair strokes for a softer result. If the only problem is a few gaps, background colour can be tattooed. The cost varies: for solid brows it's about $600, hair strokes are about $800, and small areas from $110.

2. LIPLINE, LIPLINE AND BLEND, AND FULL LIP COLOUR

Lipliner can be tattooed to define the lips or enlarge them. If the lips have been enlarged, colour can be blended from the new lipline onto part of the lips, making the outline less obvious. This technique can also be used to balance a crooked lip shape. If the natural lip colour is very pale or uneven colour can be implanted all over the lips. A large range of colours is available. The lips are highly coloured when first done but, after healing, 20 to 60 percent of the original colour is lost. The procedure is painful. One Sydney cosmetic tattoo specialist arranges for clients at her salon to have a dental injection first to numb the lips. At some other salons a topical cream is applied to deaden the surface, but probably not quite enough! If a salon does not offer the option of a dental injection, organise your own. The cost of lip tattooing ranges from about $500 to $900, depending on the amount of colour; a dental injection fee is about $80 to $100. Touch-ups are usually about a fifth of the original cost.

3. EYELINER

Applied to top and/or bottom eyelids, eyeliner tattoos can be fine or thick, or dotted in-between eyelashes to make them look thicker. Eye shadow shading above the upper line is an additional option that might be taking things too far viewed first thing in the morning. The cost is from about $500 for top or bottom liners with about $300 extra for shading.

COSMETIC TATTOOING: MIRANDA'S STORY

Miranda (60) is blond with pale lips that she wanted darkened and given new definition. 'I got sick of applying make-up, but I'm of the generation that doesn't feel right without make-up at work or if I'm going out.' She says that the lifespan (around five years) of a cosmetic tattoo is about right; a lifelong cosmetic tattoo wouldn't be desirable. 'I'll retire at 65 and won't need to wear make-up all the time.' Miranda had her lips filled-in with an edge drawn slightly outside the natural lipline, and also had eyeliner tattooed on the upper eyelids with tiny 'flick-ups' at the ends. 'At first my husband found it a little creepy waking up beside someone who looked fully made up, but now he likes it.'

Miranda also went with a girlfriend (and a bottle of wine) to an ordinary tattoo parlour and got two small rose tattoos, one above her left breast and the other above her bikini line. The cost was $80 and $120 (for one slightly larger).

NIPS AND TUCKS

Whatever the extravagant claims of
cosmetic companies, the sad truth is that only
surgery can have a significant effect on the
damage caused by the forces of gravity. Gravity is
the cause of drooping and folds around the eyes,
jawline and neck, and is associated with the
loss of skin elasticity and depleted
subcutaneous fat.

In Australia, only members of the Australian Society of
Plastic Surgeons have the recognised training necessary
to carry out complicated procedures. It takes eight to
ten years of extra training on top of a medical degree to
qualify as a plastic surgeon. You can check whether
somebody is a fully trained plastic surgeon by ringing
the society's hotline (1300 367 446) or checking the
website (www.plasticsurgery.org.au).

Fees vary widely depending on the complexity of the
procedure, but most surgeons work to a schedule
recommended by the Australian Medical Association. In
addition, there might also be fees charged by hospitals
and support practitioners such as anaesthetists. Refunds
from Medicare and private health funds vary, and if a
procedure is strictly cosmetic in most cases there is
none. It's important to discuss fees and any other costs

with your plastic surgeon at the outset. You can then check with Medicare and your private health fund.

Because of the risks involved with any surgery, plastic surgery should never be undertaken lightly or with unrealistic expectations. And all plastic surgery procedures may leave the skin very sensitive to the sun, so sunscreen should be worn at all times. Here are three of the more common cosmetic procedures:

1. EYELID LIFT (BLEPHAROPLASTY)

This surgery is performed on the upper and/or lower eyelids and is designed to remove excess skin folds and bulging fat bags. It will improve the bags and wrinkles around the eyes, but not on the cheeks, temples or forehead. The procedure can be performed as day surgery or with a short hospital stay, usually overnight, under local anaesthesia (with or without sedation) or under general anaesthesia. Usually, upper and lower eyelid incisions are marked along natural lines and extend into the crow's feet at the outer edge of the eye. Excess skin and fat are removed and the incisions closed. The procedure takes one to two hours. Scars will be kept as inconspicuous as possible, along natural skin lines and creases, and usually fade to become barely noticeable. There will be some bruising and swelling around the eyes, lasting from two to three weeks. Most patients are able to return to work after seven to ten days. The cost for both upper and lower eyelids is approximately $4000, plus hospital and anaesthetic charges.

2. FACELIFTS

The surgery undertakes to correct sagging skin. In most cases an incision, beginning in the hairline at the temple, extends along a skin crease down in front of the ear, around the ear lobe and then behind the ear, and occasionally extends to the hairline of the scalp. This gives access for the surgeon to separate skin from underlying fat and muscle. The underlying structures (muscle and connective tissue) are repositioned and the skin is then redraped mostly upwards and slightly backwards, and excess skin removed. In some cases, additional procedures such as removal of fat from under the chin and jawline are performed. Facelift surgery can take from two to four hours, and may be performed as day surgery or in hospital, under local anaesthetic or general anaesthetic. Patients will have some bruising and swelling for two or three weeks after surgery and may be aware of tightness and numbness in their face and neck. Normal make-up can be applied after seven to ten days. Most patients take two or three weeks off work. A facelift will cost between $7000 and $15 000, depending on the extent of surgery required.

3. NON-SURGICAL THREAD LIFT

Part of a new wave of cosmetic procedures, this minimally invasive surgery can be performed in less than an hour under local anaesthetic. The surgeon makes a small stab incision in the scalp tissue then uses a long, fine needle to insert special threads covered with tiny barbs into the facial tissues. The barbs open like tiny umbrellas to form a support structure that gently lifts the tissues. Over months, the body's natural production of new collagen forms around the threads, strengthening the support.

The procedure is not a radical rejuvenation, so it is suitable for people in their forties who are starting to worry about the signs of ageing, and for others in their fifties and sixties who want to lessen the effect of drooping jowls and cheeks, firm the jawline, and soften lines. It can also be used to restore the waning effects of a facelift.

The threads are made of polypropylene, which is used in brain, heart and abdominal surgery and is not reabsorbed by the body.

This may be a procedure for people who want a more dramatic result than injectable fillers or Botox (see 'Cosmeceuticals' on page 98) but who do not want a full facelift. Unfortunately its effect is normally shortlived, lasting less than a year. Costs vary according to the area(s) treated, but a jowl lift with liposuction to remove fat costs approximately $2500.

Note: Some other cosmetic surgery interventions include: liposuction ($2500 to $10 000, depending on the areas treated), breast augmentation ($5000 to $8000), filler injections ($500 to $1500, depending on the number of lines treated), nose surgery ($5000 to $6000), and tummy tuck ($6000 to $8000). All prices are rough guides only.

EYELID LIFT SURGERY: SAMANTHA'S STORY

Samantha had an eyelid lift and wrinkles under the lower lids tightened. Done under full anaesthetic, a two-hour operation with a night in a private hospital cost her about $4000. 'I had a top plastic surgeon recommended by a friend I saw before and after a similar procedure. She looked wonderful, but not too wonderful or different. It's often a problem – women have too much done and look stretched.' Samantha didn't tell anyone about the surgery. 'No one noticed except my son, who said that my eyes were sparkling.'

After the surgery, Samantha retreated to a holiday house and wore sunglasses in public for two weeks. 'I was black and blue like I'd been belted. But after two weeks I only needed make-up to cover the faint bruising. It's a good idea to have subtle cosmetic surgery done when you're on holiday, because when you return to work you just look healthy and relaxed.'

Samantha's husband was so impressed that he consulted the same surgeon and had liposuction and a thread lift on his jawline.

DRASTIC WEIGHT LOSS MEASURES

When you've tried everything you can in the areas
of diet and exercise to lose weight and failed, there
are other options. But the failure must be a true one
and not just an unwillingness to make the hard
decisions, because the alternatives are not to be
undertaken lightly.

A new procedure called VBLOC is being clinically
trialled and, if successful, will eventually become available
here. A laparoscope is inserted into the abdomen to
implant electrodes into the vagus nerve. When this nerve
is stimulated it blocks hunger signals from the brain.
During the day a small power pack is worn around the
waist to power the electrodes.

But for now, here are three of the best options
currently available to achieve drastic weight loss.

1.

Gastric banding (also known as lap banding) and bypass
procedures can be considered if you are obese (with a
Body Mass Index — see page 43 — of over 35) to the
extent that it is a danger to your health. About 7 percent
of Australians are morbidly obese (BMI of 40 or more).

Surgery for morbid obesity has been around for about 50 years, starting with jejunoileal bypass (a malabsorptive procedure) in the 1950s and followed by gastric bypass (a malabsorptive-restrictive procedure) in the 1960s. Gastric banding is a purely restrictive procedure done with a laparoscopic technique so it is less invasive than the earlier procedures. A silicone band is placed around the stomach near its upper end, creating a small pouch and a narrow passage into the larger part of the stomach. This limits the amount of food that the stomach can hold at any time, so the patient feels full with a small amount of food and will continue to feel full for several hours. The silicone band has an inflatable section filled with saline so that the size of the passage to the larger part of the stomach can be modified by injection or withdrawal of saline. This can be done as an outpatient procedure. Follow-up is important with regular exercise and good dietary habits (don't cheat with chocolates and other calorie-dense foods, or by drinking with meals as this causes food to pass into the larger part of the stomach faster).

The cost of about $5000 for gastric banding is covered in part by Medicare when patients are considered to be morbidly obese. Cost of the gastric band itself is not covered by Medicare, but some private health funds provide benefits for aids and appliances, such as gastric bands.

2.

Liposuction is a cosmetic surgical procedure to remove localised collections of fat, such as on the thighs, buttocks, abdomen, upper arms and under the chin. It is not a treatment, however, for generalised weight loss. The surgeon uses a long narrow tube (cannula) attached to a high-powered suction pump and inserts it into a small incision (about 1cm). Fat is vacuumed out of the body. More than half of our body fat stays hidden within the body while the rest, found between the muscle and the skin, is known as superficial fat. It is this superficial fat that liposuction removes. Surgical lipectomy, which involves removal of excess skin, may be advised in addition to liposuction.

Liposuction can be performed as day surgery or with an overnight stay in hospital, using local or general anaesthesia, dependent on the area to be treated and the general health of the patient. Slight skin irregularities, such as dimples and pitting, can be a side effect. A pressure garment is usually worn for two to three months to decrease bruising and swelling and to encourage the skin to shrink back. Depending on the extent of the procedure, the cost is usually between $1500 and $4500, with abdominal liposuction at the high end.

3.

Tummy tucks (abdominoplasty) and bodylifting are cosmetic surgery procedures to remove excess skin and fat from the lower abdomen which may extend onto the hips and back, and can't be exercised away. These procedures may also tighten the abdominal muscles. They are more procedures for skin laxity than obesity, and you should be at a good weight and be fit.

A full abdominoplasty is a major operation performed under general anaesthesia. An incision is made across the lower abdomen just above the pubic area that extends laterally along or above the bikini line. Another incision is made around the navel to free the surrounding skin and then all of the skin is separated from the abdominal wall. If the tummy muscles are separated (usually from pregnancy) then they are sutured together. This tightens the muscles to create a stronger abdominal wall and a smaller waist. Excess skin is removed, liposuction might be performed and a new opening is made for the navel. The procedure takes one to three hours and stays in hospital vary from one to three days. In the first few days the abdomen will feel tight and there will be pain and discomfort, hopefully controlled by medication. Scars are permanent, but generally flatten out and lighten in colour in about a year. Most people can return to work in two to four weeks and resume vigorous exercise in six weeks. The cost is around $6000 to $9000.

TUMMY TUCK SURGERY:
ELIZABETH'S STORY

Elizabeth had a tummy tuck after a botched hysterectomy that left her with an ugly scar and loose skin overhanging it. She decided to have the tummy tuck and an eyelid lift (blepharoplasty) at the same time. Doing it that way, Elizabeth saved money, spent just one night in hospital, and had one recovery period rather than two. The cost was $6000 for each procedure. 'I don't remember it being very painful. There was a lot of tightness and I was bent over for days.' She wore a special corset for weeks. 'The skin is freed from muscle during the operation and has to be held in place while it reattaches.' After five years she has a really good set of stomach muscles and a 'dead-flat tummy'. 'Because fat cells are removed by liposuction, you don't get fat back in the area – although it does go elsewhere!'

Elizabeth, now 60, has always kept fit, running marathons at one stage, and now walks a lot and goes to a gym regularly. The idea of plastic surgery wasn't new to her. Her mother, 84, has had two facelifts and an eyelid lift. 'Her partner is 12 years younger and she looks great, no one would guess her age.'

PEACE

MEDITATION TECHNIQUES

1.

The simplest way to start meditating is to sit upright with a straight spine either on a chair or on the floor (on a cushion, if you like), shut your eyes, and focus on your breathing. Don't try to push thoughts out of your mind or to control your breathing. Just concentrate on your breath as it enters the nostrils and leaves them. Incorporating a mantra (a special word or phrase) can help you focus on your breathing. Your mantra can be any word you like: it can be a word or phrase of religious significance, or something that inspires you such as 'peace' or 'calm', or the word 'om' (pronounced *aum* in eastern meditation). Try to do this for five minutes initially.

2.

Sitting in a yoga position can help you relax and concentrate. Bend the forefinger of each hand and place it on the ball of the thumb. Relax your other fingers so they are spread apart. Sit on the floor cross-legged in the lotus position (if you can manage it), with shoulders down and back so that the spine is straight. Rest the backs of your hands on the tops of your knees.

3.

Mindfulness meditation is an effective way of reducing stress and other negative feelings. The idea is to be fully engaged in the present so that your mind isn't dwelling on things that have happened in the past or that might happen in the future. A good way to try this is while taking a walk. Focus on the physicality of the experience, your feet touching the ground, your breathing, the sensation of the sun on your body, or a breeze against your face. Or try eating mindfully. Sit at the table with no distractions such as television and focus all your attention on the meal. Eat slowly and enjoy the food, concentrating on each bite. When your mind wanders bring it back to the present. Mindfulness meditation teaches us how to become more aware of our fluctuating emotions without reacting to them.

SETTING THE MOOD FOR RELAXATION

Creating the right atmosphere for relaxation is an important part of cultivating calm.

1. SET THE MOOD IN YOUR HOME

Surrounding ourselves with beautiful things isn't always possible, but it's amazing how a vase of fresh-cut flowers can lift the spirits. Scented candles, a small aromatherapy lamp with a tray of your favourite scented beads, or some favourite music are also good mood enhancers. And there are few things more relaxing than watching goldfish in a bowl or an aquarium.

2. BE AWARE OF DISTURBING INFLUENCES AND CUT DOWN ON THEM AS MUCH AS POSSIBLE

For instance, if you must have a mobile phone, don't keep it by your side at all times so that you can be reached at any time of the day or night. The same goes for a landline phone. Use an answering machine to screen calls and turn it down low when you want to focus on something important you have to do or when you want to chill out. Don't be available to everyone all the time.

3. FIND A PASTIME THAT YOU FIND RELAXING

Activities that involve a low level of concentration and soothing repetition — like knitting, swimming or doing jigsaw puzzles — are good. The mind is focused enough to drive out negative thoughts, but not stressed.

COMFORT FOODS

1. ASPARAGUS SOUP

1 leek

2 bunches asparagus

2 tablespoons olive oil

1 teaspoon salt

1 litre chicken stock

1 cup milk

Prepare the leek by cutting off the tough green part at the top. Make two crossways cuts down the length of the leek almost to the root, rinse well in a sink of water and finely slice. Break off and discard the tough ends of the asparagus (at the point where they snap easily) and slice into pieces about one-centimetre wide, leaving the tops and setting aside. Heat the oil in a pot and add the leek, cover and cook over low heat for about five minutes before adding the sliced asparagus and salt. Continue to cook covered, stirring occasionally, for 10 to 15 minutes. When the vegetables have softened, puree using a hand-held blender or food processor. Add the stock to the puree and heat through. Add the asparagus tops. (At this stage the soup can be frozen for future use if desired.) Before serving, add the milk and heat. Serves four.

2. INDIVIDUAL MACARONI CHEESES

400g macaroni
60g butter
1½ tablespoons plain flour
1½ cups milk
120g grated cheddar cheese
120g grated parmesan
black pepper
breadcrumbs
extra butter

Grease four ramekins. Preheat oven to 180°C. Bring a saucepan of salted water to the boil, add macaroni and cook until al dente. While the macaroni is cooking, melt butter in a saucepan and stir in flour, cooking and stirring for one minute. Heat milk and gradually stir into the roux (flour and butter mix). Keep stirring until the sauce is thick and smooth. Stir in cheddar cheese and parmesan and add black pepper to taste. Drain the macaroni and combine with the cheese sauce. Spoon into ramekins and sprinkle with breadcrumbs and a few dots of butter. Place in oven and cook until tops are lightly browned. Serve with green salad.

3. RHUBARB AND BERRY CRUMBLE

500g frozen rhubarb
2—3 tablespoons sugar
250g frozen cherries
250g frozen blueberries
200g plain flour
120g caster sugar
pinch of salt
120g cold diced butter

Cook frozen rhubarb with 2 or 3 tablespoons sugar (depending on taste) and enough water to cover about three-quarters of the fruit. Cook until the rhubarb starts to soften, test liquid for sweetness, then add frozen cherries and frozen blueberries. Turn off the heat. In a food processor, pulse plain flour, caster sugar and pinch of salt until combined. Add cold diced butter and pulse until crumbly. Preheat the oven to 200°C. Pour the cooked fruit into a buttered casserole dish then sprinkle the crumble mix over the fruit and bake for about 30 minutes, or until the top is browned and you can see the fruit bubbling underneath. Serve with cream or ice-cream. Serves six.

RELAXATION TECHNIQUES

These are skills and need to be practised regularly, preferably in a quiet place where you won't be disturbed.

1.

Deep breathing is the best way to start. Sit in a comfortable position with your spine straight, either in a chair or cross-legged on the floor. Put one hand on your chest and the other on your stomach. Breathe in through your nose. The hand on your stomach should rise, while the hand on your chest should move very little. Exhale through your mouth, pushing out as much air as you can while contracting your abdominal muscles. The hand on your stomach should move in as you exhale, while the other hand moves very little. If you find this difficult, try lying on the floor with a small book on your stomach, and breathe so that the book rises as you inhale and falls as you exhale. You can combine deep breathing with some aromatherapy or soothing music.

2.

Progressive muscle relaxation involves tensing each muscle group in turn, then relaxing.

Take off your shoes and lie on the floor wearing loose, comfortable clothing. Starting with your right foot, then the left, tense the muscles, squeezing as hard as you can, hold for ten seconds, then release, feeling the tension flowing away. Move up the body to the calf muscles, thigh muscles, hips and buttocks, stomach, chest, back, arms and hands, neck and shoulders, and the face, tensing the muscles then releasing.

3.

Visualising a special place is a technique that can be practised anywhere, so it can come in handy when stressful situations arise in the home or office. Imagine a scene in which you feel at peace – this is the place you will keep coming back to. It might be a beach, or a walking track through bush, or a mountain creek, anywhere that fires your imagination. Imagine it in detail, every step of the way, taking in everything you see, hear, smell and feel. Let your worries drift away as you feel at peace. If you like, make your own audio recording, speaking slowly and calmly, and use that to take you back to your special place.

SUGGESTIONS FOR RELAXING FROM BLACK DOG INSTITUTE

When tension is high and time short, here are three quick ways to calm down.

1.

Tense everything in your whole body and hold that tension as long as you can without feeling pain. Slowly release the tension and very gradually feel it leave your body. Repeat three times.

2.

Open your imagination and focus on your breathing. As your breathing becomes calm and regular, imagine that the air you inhale comes to you as a cloud — visualise the cloud in a soothing colour.

3.

With your head level and body relaxed, pick a spot to focus on. Count five breaths backward, allowing your eyes to close gradually with each breath. When you get to one, your eyes will be closed. Focus on the feeling of relaxation.

NATURAL REMEDIES FOR INSOMNIA

1. LISTEN TO AUDIO BOOKS
(USE HEADPHONES IF YOU SHARE A BED)

The idea is that listening to a book focuses the mind and distracts from problems or disturbing thoughts so that you relax and drift off to sleep, like kids do with a bedtime story. Listening to music doesn't work the same way as it won't necessarily shut out other thoughts. Most libraries have an excellent range of talking books either in tape or CD format, which will automatically switch off at the end of the side. Just make sure not to choose something creepy!

2. REALISE THAT INSOMNIA IS THE BEST CURE FOR INSOMNIA

Try to keep awake instead of trying to go to sleep. Lie on your back with the light off and keep your eyes open. As your eyelids start to droop, force them open and keep doing this until the impulse to sleep becomes irresistible.

3. DON'T WORRY TOO MUCH ABOUT IT

The more we worry and try to force ourselves to sleep, the harder it is. You may not be missing as much sleep as you think, and if you have a bad night one night you will probably sleep well the next. If you're trying to wean yourself off sleeping tablets on a doctor's advice, try halving the tablet, then try doing without it on a night when it's not as important to get a good night's sleep, for instance, on a weekend when you have nothing much on in the morning. And don't resort to taking an afternoon nap the next day — save that tired feeling for bedtime!

GETTING IN THE MOOD FOR SLEEP

1.

If you take a calcium supplement, swallow the tablet not long before you want to go to sleep. The calcium works like a glass of warm milk. Of course, you can simply have a glass of warm milk, and research indicates that adding a malt-based flavouring can put us in the mood for sleep.

2.

Tuck a lavender sachet under your pillow or dab a little lavender oil on your forehead. Or sip a cup of herbal tea after dinner: many contain ingredients such as chamomile, valerian and hops, which have a soporific effect, often with flavour-enhancing herbs such as lemongrass, lemon balm and spearmint added to the mix.

3.

Writing down things that you might otherwise lie awake thinking about is a good way of clearing the decks. If you have a lot on the next day and are worried about forgetting something, write a list. Or if you feel tortured by angry thoughts about someone, write a letter expressing your grievance, then tear it up the next morning. The act of putting thoughts down on paper can be a great mind cleanser.

DON'TS FOR INSOMNIACS

1. Don't drink tea or coffee after lunch. Both contain caffeine, a stimulant which can affect your chances of getting a good night's sleep if you suffer from insomnia. Of course, decaffeinated coffee and herbal teas are fine.
2. Don't take afternoon naps, no matter how tired you feel.
3. Don't drink alcohol after dinner. A glass before or during a meal is fine, but don't continue to drink: although it may initially relax you into nodding off quickly, the effect is short term and will result in disturbed sleep.

DE-STRESSING AT YOUR DESK

You don't need to visit a spa to enjoy the de-stressing benefits of massage.

1. SCALP SOOTHER

Place your thumbs behind your ears and spread your fingers on top of your head. Move your scalp back and forth for about twenty seconds.

2. RESTING EYES

Close your eyes and place the pads of your ring fingers under your eyebrows near the bridge of your nose. Slowly increase the pressure for five to ten seconds, then gently release. Repeat three times.

3. SHOULDER TENSION RELEASE

Reach an arm across the front of your body to your opposite shoulder. Using a circular motion, press firmly on the muscle above your shoulderblade. Repeat on the other side.

WAYS TO BE CALM BY NATURE

We don't need scientific studies to know that nature is good medicine; we feel calmer and more at peace when we get outdoors into a green environment. But there is plenty of scientific evidence to testify to the physical and psychological benefits of nature. Lower blood pressure and fewer headaches and illnesses are not the only benefits: increased greenery has also been linked to lower crime rates. A study in a Chicago public housing development found 48 percent less property crime and 56 percent less violent crime in blocks with high levels of greenery. It makes sense that greenery helps us relax and regenerate, reducing feelings of aggression. Greener playgrounds have been shown to have a positive effect on child learning too. Making the schoolyard more of a contrast to the classroom refreshes children, making them better able to concentrate during lessons. The sad thing is that many children are spending less time outdoors than their parents and grandparents did in their childhoods. We need to be aware of this and make a conscious effort to redress the situation.

1. JOIN A BUSHWALKING CLUB

or check out what your local council has to offer in the way of organised walks to learn more about your area. These are sometimes linked with local heritage groups or historical societies. Some areas have bush regeneration projects that are always in need of volunteers. Get the family involved, or it's a great way to meet new people if you are on your own.

2.

Work in your garden, but also just sit in it. If you don't have a garden, start a balcony or window box garden — it's amazing what you can grow in a small space. And encourage children to garden too by giving them their own patch or a planter box.

3.

Get to know your local parks, stroll in them, and if you work in an office, eat lunch in a park. You'll reap the benefits of this food for the soul.

EASY GREEN CHOICES

The idea of saving the planet can be overwhelming, but don't give up: try these three simple, green choices.

1. Abandon the car. Use public transport and your feet whenever you can.
2. Buy simply. Eat locally produced food that is in season and with little or no packaging.
3. Turn it off. Only keep it on if you need it – lights, air conditioning and appliances.

RECYCLING

1. Organs. Go to www.medicareaustralia.gov.au to register as an organ donor.
2. Pets. Contact your local animal welfare shelter for your new best friend.
3. Waste. Most households produce just over 15 kilograms of waste each week. Recycle clean paper, plastics (PET 1, 2 and 3) aluminium and steel cans, and glass (remove the lids). Buy toilet, writing and wrapping paper on its way around again.

REASONS TO BE CLUTTER-FREE

Here are three sound reasons to bring order to your life and home. Give it a go: you can always revert to type if you don't like the new regime. Who knows, you might like sleeping in your bed when you have recycled all the old magazines currently living there!

1. CLEAR LIVING SPACE MEANS CLEAR HEAD SPACE

There are very few people who work well in clutter; they love their messy desk and know where everything is. They become frantic if anyone tries to clean up on their behalf and feel that their creativity has been thwarted and their domain violated. But the vast majority of people function better and feel better when there is order on their desk, in their wardrobe and around the house.

2. YOUR CLUTTER IS A HEALTH HAZARD

Physically and mentally, clutter can be bad for you. There is a link between clutter and allergies; sinus and asthma in particular can be triggered by dust mites and mould. If your life looks like it is out of control, sometimes it's because it is. People are mentally weighed down by the amount of debris around them. In fact, it's very hard to enjoy the moment or plan for the future if you are living in the residue of clothes that don't fit and belongings you don't need. Clutter can make you feel overwhelmed and even depressed.

3. YOUR CLUTTER IS A BURDEN

If you live with a person who doesn't like clutter, then clinging to it affects that relationship. If you lose accounts, forget important dates or misplace personal items, your clutter is costing you time and money. People who live in clutter buy more than they need and don't use what they own effectively. If the burden of fixing it all up is too much to contemplate, don't think about ridding the whole house of clutter — start with a wardrobe or a drawer. The following Three of the Best tips focus on zones in your life, rather than whole rooms, to get you started.

STEPS TO A CLUTTER-FREE WARDROBE

1. CLEAN OUT

Take out all the hanging clothes in your wardrobe and put them on an ironing board that you have set up in your bedroom. (Don't use the bed; it might be difficult sleeping that night if you run out of steam.) Wipe down the inside of the wardrobe with a dampened cloth. Get rid of wire hangers and invest in some sturdy plastic ones. Get a box for your favourite charity and air the wardrobe while you turn to the ironing board with gusto.

2. SORT OUT

Pick up each item and try to remember when you last wore it. If it was more than 12 months ago, put it in the charity box. Professional organiser, guru and author of *It's All Too Much*, Peter Walsh, recommends the 'Reverse Clothes Hanger' trick. This involves hanging all your clothes with the hangers back to front and only turning them around when you have actually worn those clothes. In six months time you will see what you never wear and don't need.

Don't keep clothes because:

- they remind you of good times (with the exception of your wedding dress, clothes are not time capsules or photographs)
- they were a bargain (if you never wear it, it never was)
- they might fit you when you drop two dress sizes (if you need to, you will, but not because of an old pair of shorts)
- 'you can never have too many …' (in fact, you can – you can only wear so many black T-shirts and underpants)
- 'it cost a lot/is a good label/is great quality' (if it is but you're not wearing it, give it to someone who will).

3. CLEANSED

By the end of your clean-out you will have:

- A box of clothes for your favourite charity.
- A wardrobe with only clothes that fit and that you love to wear. Arrange them by type so that the pants hang together, the shirts hang together, and so on, and then group for season (warm and cool).
- A small pile on the ironing board of clothes that need buttons put on, hems fixed or special treatment. If that favourite white shirt has succumbed to a bout of yellowing, try adding a small amount of white vinegar to the final wash rinse and line-drying in direct sun.

Do the same Three of the Best steps for:

- folded items (a drawer each for underwear, knits, pyjamas and so on)
- shoes (think about shoe trees for expensive pairs and sort out if there are resoling and polishing jobs to be done)
- handbags (put expensive ones in bags; an easy option is an old pillowcase).

STEPS TO A CLUTTER-FREE KITCHEN

1. CLEAN OUT

Some clutter jobs are scorched-earth in approach; you have to pull out everything to start with. If you take that approach in the kitchen you will never start. Instead, do the kitchen cupboards drawer by drawer and shelf by shelf. When you have a spare ten minutes, start with the utensil drawer. Get your charity box and throw-out box ready. Don't put anything back in the drawer/shelf that you haven't used in the last 12 months.

The only exceptions to the 12-month rule are those special items that you use for dinner parties or big celebrations, like the nice glassware or Aunt Mavis's silver service. You should ask yourself if you are ever going to use them or perhaps, better still, if you could use them on a weekly basis and get more enjoyment out of them. Wipe out all the cleared surfaces with warm soapy water.

2. CLEAR OUT

If storage space is a real issue in the kitchen or drawers are so messy you can never find anything, invest in some drawer organisers or shelf stands so you can sort and stack everyday items. Ikea has a good range, as do large hardware stores. Keep the plates, bowls and glasses in the easiest to reach areas near the most used bench space. Have one space for plastic storage, one space for pots and pans and separate shelving for foodstuffs.

Find other places for less essential items. Could those cookbooks live on the bookshelf? Could the vases live in the laundry? Is the garage cool enough to be the wine cellar? The kitchen will function better if you really streamline the equipment into every day and every week use. If you never use the fondue set, breadmaker or the tagine pot, give it to someone who will.

Everyone needs a junk drawer — just don't make it a drawer. Buy a plastic tub about the dimensions of a shoe box and use it for spare laces, batteries, globes and elastic bands. Don't let it grow by pruning regularly.

3. SET UP

Once you have prioritised your utensils and the space they live in, think about any space that is left over. Do you have room for a box for paper and glass recycling? Do you have enough space to grow herbs on the bench? Is there a spare wall for a family whiteboard? What about the fire extinguisher or fire blanket? This is not an exercise about bringing in more debris to replace the stuff you have just got rid of, but more about making the kitchen a good place to be. In terms of family time, people tend to spend most of it in the kitchen and it is often the control centre of the home. Make sure it works well for you.

STEPS TO A CLUTTER-FREE LINEN CUPBOARD

1. CLEAN OUT

Take everything out of the linen cupboard. In an ideal world it should only store linen, blankets, doonas, towels, bath mats and your grandmother's tablecloth. Sometimes it becomes a catch-all for other goodies. Now is probably a good time to confront those interlopers (the old school project and the spare backpack). If there is something in the linen press that isn't linen, you probably don't need it. Wipe out the shelving with a damp cloth, dry and air. Get out the charity box.

2. SORT OUT

Go through all the items and weed out the worn-out. If you wouldn't use a towel or sheet for a house guest, then it is time to give it to a charity that recycles for rags. If you are hiding behind notions of using old sheets for painting or old towels for washing the dog, put them in the garage or laundry. If space is an issue you can buy vacuum bags which compress the doonas and blankets. This will also keep them dust-free. It's a good idea to keep your blankets in bags – often their original packaging will do the trick – to keep dust mites at bay.

3. CLEANSED

Restock your cupboard with a system that works for you; perhaps all bathroom stock on one shelf, all sheets on another. If you are ironing your sheets you have the nation's permission to stop now. If you can't, just do the pillowcases.

Tame those fitted sheets by folding them well. Put the fitted sheet flat on a hard surface with the elasticized side facing up. Take two corners and tuck those corners inside the other corners. The sheet is now in half. Fold in half again and again until you have a neat package.

Put together a bowl of potpourri for your clutter-free cupboard — experiment with rose petals, dried lemon peel, lavender flowers, eucalyptus leaves and cloves.

STEPS TO A CLUTTER-FREE BATHROOM CUPBOARD

1. CLEAN OUT

Take everything out of the bathroom cupboard. Get a box for the throw-outs. Wipe out the cupboard with warm water and dry thoroughly.

2. THROW OUT

Separate the medications from the beauty products. Check both groups for expiry dates, especially the meds. If you haven't used a beauty product in 12 months then you are never going to use it. Put the dead-from-neglect items in the throw-out box. All cosmetics and perfumes have a limited life span. Beauty products should display a small drawing of a tub with '12M' or '24M' marked inside, indicating a shelf life or one or two years. Others with a more limited life span will sport a 'best before' date. Lipsticks are good for about one year; mascara, eye shadow, eyeliner and blush less than that. Nail polish can be kept successfully for two years. Most importantly, sunscreen should be replaced every three years, earlier if the colour or odour changes. Perfume is generally good for three years. Make sure the storage area is cool and dry.

Put the medications in a childproof plastic container. If you have the space to store them somewhere else, such as a top shelf in the laundry or kitchen, then that will be safer than with alluring beauty products.

3. CLEANSED

Put back your everyday items on the eye-level shelf. If you have loose lipsticks, mascaras and other tools of trade, get some small plastic boxes and create a make-up artist's kit in your cupboard.

STEPS TO CLEAN OUT YOUR BOOKSHELVES

1. CLEAR OUT

Take all your books off the shelf. Some de-cluttering jobs can be done piecemeal – this is not one of them. Wipe down all the shelving and dry well. Silverfish and mildew need moisture to survive, so make sure the area is dry and well ventilated.

2. CLEAN OUT

Get two boxes and in one put all the books that are damaged to the point that no one will ever want to read them. That box is for the recycling bin. In the other box put the books that you no longer have any interest in and put it in your car. Drop it off to a charity that takes household goods, such as Lifeline or the Salvation Army.

3. CLEANSED

Put all the remaining books back on the shelves in an order that makes sense to you:

- subject matter
- author
- fiction/non-fiction

If your books are suffering from a bout of mildew, wipe down the covers with a soft cloth dampened with warm water and washing-up detergent before wiping dry. If the inside papers are also mouldy, spread the books like a fan in the sun and let them 'burn' for a day. Talcum powder might do the trick in an extreme case.

STEPS TO A CLUTTER-FREE GARAGE

This is the hardest area in the house to make clutter-free. Everything about the garage cries out for hoarding: it's big, you can avoid looking at it, guests don't generally venture in and nobody feels they 'own' the mess. You will have to be brave to take on the garage. On a positive note, you can enlist the whole family to help. Whilst cleaning your underwear drawer is personal and best done with a glass of red on a winter's afternoon, the garage is a family affair which can generate togetherness. The same principles can be applied to the attic or basement or backyard shed (although there may be some emotional attachment to the contents of the latter by your partner).

1. CLEAN OUT

Move the car into the driveway and open the boot. Start with the pile closest to the car; hold up the slightly decomposed wetsuit and get the family to try to think of a reason why you should keep it. There won't be one because there are only two questions to ask in the garage:

- Did you use it in the last twelve months?
- Would you use it again in its current state?

If the answer to either of those questions is no, put it straight into the car.

You might want to divide the boot into two areas: one for the tip and one for the charity bin. And there might be another pile for the garage sale; indeed you might want to add all your clothes, books and other household goodies that you have already sorted into that pile. (No doubt you have already spotted the danger of this approach – have a look at 'Steps to a successful garage sale' on page 157, before making a garage sale pile.)

2. SORT OUT

After you have gone through each item, all that should be left in the garage is a modest pile of items that you use on a year-in, year-out basis: the esky, the bike, the tent, the spare tiles for the roof and so on. Buy some big plastic tubs (put labels on them) or shelving for smaller items. Some expensive items like surfboards are worth suspending off the wall or ceiling. Your hardware shop has lots of useful hooks and hangers.

3. CLEANSED

When the boot is full, delegate the tip/charity bin drop-off to one member of the family. Now that the floor space is clear, sweep up. You might want to buy a second-hand vacuum cleaner to keep the floor in a good state. Some people discover enough floor space to set up a small home gym; you could get yourself a set of handweights or a boxing bag. Diarise the job in another six months; it will never be that hard again.

STEPS TO A SUCCESSFUL GARAGE SALE

1. GEAR UP

Pick a weekend in the near future for your garage sale. Plan to start early and finish early — keen garage sale junkies will be visiting garages all day, so it pays to be one of the first sites when enthusiasm and cash running high. In the preceeding 24 hours, post some signs around your neighbourhood to advertise the address and starting time. Some local councils don't appreciate the electricity poles being decorated, so it is worth checking before you put up signs. You can place a notice in your local paper, do a letterbox drop or use www.egaragesales.com.au to place an advertisement (this website also has free printable signs).

2. SET UP

The day before the sale, make sure your items are clean and sorted into groups according to price or description. The better the display, the better the appeal. Put prices on items; generally most should be between $2 and $10, although buyers will soon tell you what they think it is worth! Be prepared to reduce prices to move your stock.

Set up your sale station with lots of spare change, drinks, snacks and a buddy for support.

3. CLEAN UP

An hour before your nominated pack-up time, make an effort to reduce prices and sell as much as you can. If you have encouraged buyers to come back at the end of the day for a bargain, be prepared to give them one. Make up groups of items for a bargain price.

When it's all over, take the rest to your favourite charity who deal in household goods. St Vincent de Paul and the Salvation Army will pick up furniture by arrangement. Don't take anything back into the house; temporary lodgings only in the garage. Take down any neighbourhood signs before you count your earnings.

CLEANING IDEAS FOR A SPARE 10, 30 OR 60 MINUTES

1. Ten minutes. Identify the most unruly drawer in your house – underwear? kitchen utensils? desk? – and clean it out.

2. Thirty minutes. Do a house speed-clean. Pick up anything that is on the floor and looks abandoned, such as dirty clothes, newspapers and shoes. Wipe down or vacuum every unencumbered surface that is larger than a pillowcase. Clean the toilet, the bathroom basin and the kitchen sink, including taps. You're done.

3. Sixty minutes. Save your backyard from death by neglect. If it is large, divide it up into four sections and do one section today. Get a hessian sack or a box and string. With gloves and secateurs, put weeds in the sack or box and tie up cut branches. Plan your four-pronged attack to coincide with the next council clean-up. Most councils have garden clean-ups as well as general clean-ups. Ring and ask them.

BEATING THE BLUES

Everyone has bad days. If those bad days are accumulating into weeks, you might be more than just a bit blue. Do an online search for the Edinburgh Depression Scale; it will tell you if you have the symptoms of depression. For a diagnosis you should see your doctor or another health-care professional. If you think you could be suffering from antenatal or postnatal depression (and more than 10 percent of pregnant woman and mothers in Australia do), the scale is a good first base for you too. To ward off the temporary miseries, try these Three of the Best.

1. THINK ABOUT OTHERS

Is there a friend who could do with your help at the moment? Someone who would appreciate some home-cooked meals delivered to their door, some babysitting or their garden cleaned up?

If no one comes to mind, think about volunteer work. Have a look at websites such as www.fido.com.au or www.govolunteer.com.au. Both are not-for profit and can match your skills to an organisation that will really appreciate your input.

2. KEEP BUSY

Don't lie in bed or hang around the house. Be active and engage with other people — both are blues-blocker strategies. Ring up a friend and organise a get-together. Try a power walk with a buddy and try to make it a weekly event as exercise is a great mood enhancer. If you are on your own, keep mentally busy: don't do housework or mindless gardening as you will soon be dwelling on your woes. Put an elastic band around your wrist — every time your mind reverts to your sad state of affairs, give the band a twang and move on to a positive thought.

3. HAPPINESS IS AN ACT OF WILL

Write down the activities and people who make you happy. Think about a sport you did as a child that you really liked. Think about the people who make you feel positive and energised. Already you have a plan of things to do and people to meet. Don't wait for contentment to fall into your lap: plan for it. Think about things you can do today, next week and next holiday that will make you feel good about yourself. Don't think that everything will be better when you have a) lost weight; b) found a partner or c) got a better job. Write a realistic plan about how to start achieving your goals now and enjoy the fact that you are already on the right road.

WAYS TO GIVE

It not only helps others, it makes you feel better too.

1. Blood. Donate regularly by contacting www.donateblood.com.au.

2. Sweat. If you have any free time and like a bit of outdoor exercise, contact your council for details on bush regeneration projects in your area. If there is nothing organised, find a bit of local turf that looks neglected and contact your council with a proposal for improvement.

3. Tears. Training is provided for telephone counselling by Lifeline (www.wesleymission.org.au) and the Salvation Army (www.salvos.org.au).

MAKING YOUR LIFE SIMPLER

Less is more (time, contentment and peace). Here are the Three of the Best ways to achieve it. Try it for a month and see if your life is better for it.

1. LESS TECHNOLOGY

Do you need all your 'techno-weapons'? Cut down on multiple phones, faxes, pagers and email. Do you need to watch as much television? Circle your three favourite shows each week in the paper and keep it off in-between. Are you a slave to your in-box? Check emails once a day, delete copied messages and answer as much as you can in three lines straight away. Are you a slave to your phone? Use an answering service at home and field your calls. If you are on holidays, ignore the computer and the phone.

Less technology means less 'fast-food' information, so while you're on a roll, cancel all but one of your magazine subscriptions, read one newspaper a day and cut off all junk mail invasions.

2. LESS SHOPPING

Eat more of what comes out of the ground (vegetables, fruits, nuts and grains). Try buying it locally and give yourself a break from monotonous supermarket expeditions. Set aside one day a month to stock up on the supermarket lines that you can't do without; toilet paper, soap, chocolate and all the other essential items on the running list that you have been keeping.

Keep another list for those shopping centre must-haves like school supplies, health-fund claims and new underpants. Wait until you have 12 items on the list before you expend your energy and petrol.

After you have made your wardrobe clutter-free and organised (see 'Steps to a clutter-free wardrobe' on page 146), you'll probably find you have more clothes to wear, not less. Make a list of any items you need to make your pieces work together, maybe a white shirt or black pants, and then have a rest from clothes shopping for a while.

If you do less shopping, you'll have less stuff. Less to pay for, clean, take care of, insure, worry about and replace.

3. LESS WORK

Not everyone can work four days a week instead of five, but have a look at www.workplace.gov.au. Go to the 'Work life balance' page where you'll find useful fact sheets on how to develop a family-friendly work environment and flexible work arrangements. Could you put together a proposal for your boss's consideration? Try to timetable a weekend that doesn't involve work, whether it is of the paid or household variety. Make it a time for family or friends or interests that have a positive impact on you.

Try to get away by public transport or a short drive for a weekend with only hand luggage. Always use your holiday entitlements; people who collect them like medals look like the walking wounded in the office.

Aim to have your lunch outside for fresh air and exercise.

Get up a bit earlier and do some exercise before work, or leave on time and try out the nearest gym.

WORK–LIFE BALANCE

Linda Duxbury, a professor at Carleton University's Sprott School of Business in Ottawa, Canada, is an authority on the work–family juggle after conducting groundbreaking studies of 33,000 Canadians in 1991 and another 37,000 in 2001. In an interview published in the *Sydney Morning Herald*, 23 April 2008 she revealed that she has no mobile phone or BlackBerry, refuses to answer calls during dinner, never works on weekends or holidays, and takes a three-day break away with her family once a month. Presenting the findings of a study of about 13,000 Australians working in professions, she said that more than half the respondents worked more than 48 hours a week. And while Linda admits to doing that herself, by drawing a line between work and home she has achieved a balance. To get that balance in our own lives:

1.

Work hard at the office, but learn to leave it behind.

2.

Recognise what is important in your life. Sometimes climbing the ladder in a job can take you away from the work you enjoy to a more stressful lifestyle. So think carefully about where you want to end up. In 1999, economist and Nobel prize-winner Daniel Kahneman demonstrated through studies at Princeton University that what we think will make us happy, such as higher income, is not related to levels of happiness.

3.

Take proper holidays and weekend getaways and don't let work intrude.

ON GENERATIONAL CHANGE

Can't maintain a peaceful communication? This might be why.

1. Baby Boomers: born 1946–1964
2. Gen X: born 1965–1979
3. Gen Y: born after 1980

WAYS TO PROTECT YOUR PRIVACY

1.

Most of us prefer not to be annoyed by telemarketers and it's easy to lock them out. Simply make a free call to 1300 792 958 on your own phone and telemarketers will stop calling within a few weeks. There are a few exceptions: charities are exempt and politicians can still ring to solicit your vote. You can also register on the net by going to www.donotcall.gov.au.

2.

There may be situations where you wish to block caller ID: when sussing out a prospect from an internet dating site, for instance, or seeking information anonymously. Just dial 1831 before the number you are calling and the receiver will not be able to identify yours.

3.

Be careful about giving out your email address to avoid ending up on mailing lists. Spam (junk email) is now illegal in Australia – the *Spam Act 2003* came into effect on 10 April 2004 – so it is now illegal to send, or cause to be sent, unsolicited commercial electronic messages.

If you've given your email address to any commercial interest, such as a direct mail-order company, and want to opt out of further email communications, simply click to indicate your wish to the sender and you will not be bothered again. Senders have to include an escape option with every communication.

IMPROVING YOUR MEMORY

It would be nice to have a photographic memory, but very few of us do. We need to make a conscious effort to remember things. This means paying attention and concentrating when we are told something that we need to file away. It's all too easy for information to go in one ear and out the other. Without making that conscious effort to pay attention and concentrate we have no chance of remembering.

It's common to forget names seconds after we are introduced to people, which is embarrassing if we are spending an evening together. In this situation, simply repeating the name can help, as in: 'Good to meet you, Tom.'

Without a photographic memory it's harder to remember abstract information, such as numbers. In the case of phone numbers, it helps to focus on the digits without distractions for a few minutes. Write them down in your contact book; at least you have a written record if you forget it, but the act of writing something down reinforces memory. Of course, it's not necessary to remember everything — that's why we have memory dial! But the problem with aids like that is that we can become mentally lazy simply because we don't have to test our memories.

The brain processes information in different ways. We have short-term memory, which stores information for a few minutes or a few days, but not for the longer term. It might be the dishes on a restaurant menu so we can decide what to order, or the prices of goods on the supermarket shelf. Long-term memory involves information we need to retain, such as material we need to learn for an exam, the rules of the road, even the night the garbage goes out, as well as all the facts we store away about our family and friends and the skills involved in our job. This is the information we need to lock in. Here are Three of the Best ways to improve memory:

1.

The brain is not a muscle, but regularly exercising it spurs the development of new nerve connections that can help improve memory. Challenging your brain with puzzles and games and learning new skills, such as a foreign language or musical instrument, helps keep your brain active. You can also stimulate your brain by tackling routine tasks in a different way, for instance, brushing your teeth or writing something with your non-dominant hand, or getting dressed with your eyes closed (check the mirror after, though). Exercising your body also helps by increasing oxygen to the brain and reducing the risk of diseases that can lead to memory loss, such as diabetes and cardiovascular disease.

2.

Mnemonics are clues that help us remember things, usually by linking them with an image, a word, a sentence or a rhyme. We remember the days in each month by thinking, 'Thirty days hath September, April, June and November …' And music students memorise the lines of the treble staff with the sentence, '*Every Good Boy Deserves Fruit*'. The spaces between the lines on the treble staff form the word *FACE*. We remember the planets in order of distance from the sun with the sentence, 'My very elderly mother just sits under the North Pole' (Mercury, Venus, Earth, Mars, Jupiter, Saturn, Uranus, Neptune, Pluto – although Pluto is no longer classed as a planet, which spoils that a bit). You can create your own memory triggers using word associations and visual images.

3.

Focus on understanding basic ideas. Think of yourself as a teacher having to explain complex ideas to someone else. Work out the best way to do this simply and clearly and imprint it in your mind.

WAYS TO GET ORGANISED SO YOU DON'T FORGET

1.

Keep a diary with notes of all appointments, birthdays (enter these at the start of the year), bills due for payment, medical checks, and anything else you need to remember. Look at it every day; it's not much good if you don't check on a daily basis.

2.

Keep a running shopping list and take it with you whenever you go to the shops. A block pad, preferably with pencil attached, stuck with a magnet to the fridge works well.

3.

Have fixed places where you keep keys, glasses, and anything else you lose regularly.

HEALTH AIDS TO MEMORY

1. GET PLENTY OF SLEEP

A Harvard University study formally showed the benefits of sleep to memory, but it's obvious that feeling tired makes it hard to concentrate, and concentration is essential to memorising.

2. KEEP STRESS UNDER CONTROL

The stress hormone cortisol can damage the hippo-campus, a part of the brain vital in processing information as memory.

3. DON'T SMOKE

Smoking increases the risk of vascular disorders that can cause stroke and constrict arteries that deliver oxygen to the brain.

FOODS AND SUPPLEMENTS THAT CAN HELP MEMORY

1.

Antioxidants fight free radicals, which can damage cells, and they also improve the flow of oxygen though the body.

2.

Omega-3 fatty acids help brain function. Fish is the best source and we should eat at least two serves a week, but preferably more. If you don't eat fish, take a supplement.

3.

Vitamin B helps us to cope with stress and keep our minds clear. Eat lots of dark leafy greens and a variety of other fruits and vegetables as part of a well-balanced diet. Liver and kidneys are rich sources of vitamin B12; liver, dried yeast and yeast extract are excellent sources of folic acid; and fish, lentils, bananas, meat, avocados and nuts are among the best sources of vitamin B6. If you take a supplement, make it a slow-release vitamin B complex tablet containing B6, B12 and folic acid.

TIME SAVERS

Being organised can save hours every week and promote peace of mind.

1. WRITE LISTS

For a start, keep a running shopping list stuck to the fridge or in some other place where it won't get lost. Write what you need as it occurs to you or when something starts to run out, then do one shop a week – you may even be able to stretch it to once a fortnight. Make lists as daily entries in your diary, so you know what you have to do each day. Allocate one day a month for paying bills that are due and do them all at once.

2. PERSONAL EMAILS AND PHONE CALLS CAN BE A TIME WASTER WHEN YOU'RE TRYING TO WORK

Get an answering machine so that you decide whether or not to take untimely phone calls. Don't keep checking personal emails – check once or twice a day and if a reply is called for, do it straight away. Dump junk emails immediately.

3. ALWAYS CARRY SOME READING MATTER

so that you have something to do if you're taking public transport or sitting in a waiting room. It's a stress-free way of doing two things at once, plus it makes you feel more relaxed if your bus is running late or your appointment is delayed.

MONEY TIPS

Money worries can keep us awake at night, destroying all prospects of a peaceful night's sleep. You can always refer to 'Natural remedies for insomnia' on page 138, but here are Three of the Best ways to avoid money problems in the first place.

1.

Avoid the debt trap by shopping smartly. Here are some ideas:

- Write out a shopping list and stick to it.
- Don't overspend on any purchase.
- Compare prices between different stores – for major purchases you can do this on the phone before leaving the house.

- Keep all receipts, check warranties and file them in a safe place.
- Don't buy on impulse.
- If you're not sure about making a purchase, don't.
- Don't go into debt to make a purchase.
- Many stores still have lay-by, even though they don't promote it and prefer you to use store charge cards. Check it out and read terms and conditions carefully.
- Bring your own lunch from home and keep your own supply of tea and coffee in the office if your employer doesn't.
- Borrow books, audiotapes, CDs and DVDs from your local library. You can order new books you want to read at most public libraries by paying only a small fee.

2.

Budgeting requires self-discipline, but it's essential for ensuring you achieve long-term goals. For a start, it's important to know how much you are spending now. Track your spending for a month, writing down every cent of expenditure. This enables you to work out your spending pattern and see how much is necessary and how much unnecessary. Work out your exact income after regular monthly payments such as mortgage, insurance, car loan, and so on have been deducted. Then average out each month's expenditure on costs such as utilities, council rates and phone and allow for that. Remember to factor in the unexpected, such as car repairs, school excursions, household repairs, gifts, entertainment.

Once you have a clear idea of where your money is going you can identify areas where you can cut back and savings you can make. It might help to use envelopes to set aside sums for specific purposes.

Think carefully before you commit to any regular monthly payments that may not be strictly necessary, for instance, signing up for a mobile phone on a long-term plan. Mobiles eat money. Do you really need to talk on a phone in the street or sitting on a bus? If you must have a mobile, be wary of signing any contract and make sure the service exactly fits your needs. If you don't feel comfortable signing up for two years then try a prepaid service first. Instead of being tied by a contract you will be stuck with the service only until the recharge card runs out.

Signing up for cable television adds another monthly expense that you should think carefully about. If it is providing cheap entertainment for your family in place of trips to the movies and renting DVDs, that's fine, but don't commit lightly.

Also, if you have a cheap dial-up internet plan, think twice before switching to the more expensive broadband. If you never download anything other than text and a few pictures, the speed of broadband is unnecessary.

Cancel your gym membership unless you are getting real value out of it. See the Fit section for tips on getting yourself in shape without additional expenditure.

Write down your budget and stick to it. Keep long-term goals such as having enough for a deposit on a house, travelling overseas or buying a car in mind. It will make budgeting seem worthwhile. If you are budgeting because of debts, work out a plan for paying them off. Prioritise debts in order of importance. For instance: 1) rent or mortgage, because it's essential to keep the roof over your head, 2) utilities, 3) car payment, if you need a car for your job, 4) secured debts, or loans on which you have signed collateral such as your car or house, 5) unsecured debt, such as credit cards, doctors' bills, or loans from family or friends. Think about ways you can make some extra money, for example, take a second job, or sell something.

3.

The trouble with credit cards is that they distance us from the reality of spending. We can kid ourselves that we keep them as a convenience to save carrying a lot of cash around for that unexpected purchase, but using Eftpos serves that purpose. Better still, by using Eftpos we are spending money we actually have as opposed to using money we don't have and which we will eventually have to pay back with interest (unless debt is cleared before the end of the billing month). When we use Eftpos we have a totally different mindset; we are forced to think about the state of our bank balance. Of course, it's hard to get by in life without a credit card. Some regular bills have to be paid by credit card, and you need one for making phone and online purchases, booking a holiday house or motel room, and so on. But we need to make credit cards work for us rather than us working for them. Here are some tips:

a. Try to pay as much off the balance as you can at the end of the month. The best way to use a credit card is to go for one with an interest-free period and pay it off in full each month. But if you are going to carry some debt from month to month, go for one without the interest-free period but with a lower interest rate.

b. Stick to one card and don't be tempted by offers of store cards − it's easier to manage one card efficiently.

c. Don't let the bank raise your credit limit to an unmanageable level. Make sure that they don't do this on the basis that the limit is raised unless you say otherwise. Many organisations are now achieving their desired outcomes by requiring customers to specifically opt out from limit increases, rather than asking them to agree or do nothing if they don't.

Credit help lines:

· NSW: 1800 808 488
· Vic: 03 9602 3800
· WA: 08 9221 9411
· Tas: 1800 232 500

THREE OF THE BEST FOR HAVING MORE TIME

As women, we spend a lot of time worrying about getting things done on time both at work and in the home. In fact we spend a lot of the day rushing to achieve the deadlines that other people have imposed on us or that we impose on ourselves. When we are not rushing we are waiting while other people rush around. Despite all that rushing we seem to have less free time. Despite all that waiting we don't feel calm. Here are Three of the Best Strategies for getting through what you have to so you can reclaim some peace of mind.

1. LEARN TO WRITE IT DOWN

Getting your thoughts of what you have to do out of your head and onto paper, means your mind is liberated to actually do what has to be done. The self-help guru David Allen, in his book *Getting Things Done*, outlines the five keys to improved productivity whether you are home struggling to cope or in a corporation with work flow concerns. The theory is that your brain is not geared for holding onto commitment data but will do so until there is a better system on offer. You spend large amounts of time worrying about remembering to do things without actually getting things done resulting in a loss of control and perspective. The aim is to 'clarify, capture and organise' your commitments.

The five keys are: 1. Collect your jobs; 2. Process your jobs by putting them in a notebook or on screen (have a look at www.mindmeister.com); 3. Organise them into action plans such as Things to do today, Calls to make, Emails to send and so on; 4.Review them each day; and 5. Do the jobs. Do those tasks that will take less than 2 minutes straight away. The goal is to get through the immediate jobs so your mind is liberated to think about the bigger picture projects and goals (which can also be written down).

2. LEARN TO DELEGATE

Delegation at work can be problematic unless there are clear lines of authority which allow you to give work to someone else. If you are struggling, make a schedule of work; write down the pressing jobs, what it would take to complete them including any special conditions, how long it will take to complete them and the deadlines. Take a copy of your schedule to the boss and ask for 10 minutes to go through the schedule to discuss whether someone else in the organisation could help you. Even if you don't get any support, at least you now have a document to help you prioritise your work.

On the home front, there is a good chance that you are doing 70-80 per cent of the housework, parenting and domestic administration. Write down tasks that you are under pressure to get done and think about whether your partner, children or other relative could be helping you more. Children should be involved in age-appropriate household jobs; in fact it is just as important as school homework. Lots of jobs are child-friendly: vacuuming, dusting, stripping beds, gardening, feeding pets, cleaning tiles, recycling duty, hanging out washing, preparing meals, sweeping and pet care. Work out a timetable with each child and link it with any pocket money distribution. Spend time giving on-the-spot training. Give your children a sense of responsibility with their own possessions. Instead of folding and putting away their washing put it straight from the clothes line into your child's sorting tub. Then if they yell out 'Where are my jeans', you can yell back 'In your tub'.

Set up a timetable with your partner to alternate for cooking dinner, washing up, making the bed, weekend children's sport and food shopping.

Could your mother or mother-in-law be helping with school projects or school pick-ups? Would your younger brother like a gardening job to help out with student expenses?

Sit down and write down all the weekly jobs that are making your life less pleasant and/or productive, think creatively to share the load. After all apart from childbirth you weren't genetically engineered specifically for any of them.

3. LEARN TO SAY NO

A lot of women, especially in certain age groups, have enormous difficulty in saying they won't be able to do something for someone else. If they do manage to say No, they feel so guilty afterwards they wished they had said Yes. Often, as female children, we have been brought up to please other people and saying Yes to every demand and request is habitual.

You have a right to say No. Learn to say it politely and succinctly. A lot of us can't say No without a long-winded expose of our life story. You don't need to be constantly justifying yourself; just say No with a one sentence reason: 'No. I won't be able to help with the fundraiser this time because I have an upcoming work deadline.'

Avoid saying 'I'll get back to you on that' or 'I might be there'. Resolving the issue later just wastes everyone's time and is emotionally draining. People will respect you if you make your position clear and stick to it. If you have a work or home schedule written down you will know exactly what your commitments are and not take on tasks that you can't cope with.

If you really don't feel you can say No, set out what you can do clearly with boundaries: 'I can give you one hour on Friday afternoon.'

Learn to say No to some of your self-imposed commitments that don't make you happy. Clean the bathroom once a fortnight instead of once a week. Involve the children in no more than two after-school activities a week not five. Make curries and stews in double quantities and 'cook' once every two days (try 'Massaman curry' on page 313). These self-imposed commitments can be harder to refuse because they have become rituals in your life. Write them down to deal with them.

PEACEFUL CHRISTMAS SHOPPING

Christmas shopping can be very stressful: you have a large amount of shopping to do by a certain day and subject to public scrutiny, at a time of year when your budget is already under pressure due to the cost of food, drink, entertaining and holidays. Don't go into debt for Christmas: start early and use lay-by rather than credit. Think earlier and smaller and all will be jolly.

1. SHOP IN JULY

Some people might tell you how much more festive it is to shop in the lead up to Christmas, when the stores are decorated and Christmas songs replace background music.

But there is nothing festive about commercial Christmas shopping, and this is particularly true the closer you get to the big day.

Try to set aside some time mid-year to do your Christmas shopping. Write a list and go to the mid-year sales. Obviously it won't work if you are set on buying Aunt Maude an up-to-the-minute bikini for Christmas and only winter coats are available, but this is the exception rather than the rule. The idea is to get as much Christmas shopping done as is feasible before December. You will save at sales, avoid parking and shopping queues and genuinely enjoy wrapping the presents at Christmas time.

2. THINK SMALLER

Christmas is a big event, but that doesn't mean your presents have to be big. You can make or cook presents (see page 335 for recipes). You can decide with your family that each person will buy a present for another designated family member, rather than everyone buying a present for everyone else. You might decide with your extended family that the focus will be on children and the adults will have a present-free year. Or you might agree with adult family members to set a monetary limit on gifts or to buy gifts from charities. Through Oxfam, for example, you can donate seeds, animals, clothing and medicines for underprivileged communities for modest amounts and give an explanatory card as a Christmas gift: all your gifts from one shop. Arrange for overseas relatives to buy locally on your behalf and save yourself the queue at the post office and the expense of heavy postage. Make up a 'voucher' to babysit your friend's children while she goes out to dinner, or make up some hampers (perhaps teas or coffee with a mug and chocolates).

This approach will mean you need to undertake some diplomatic discussions about present-giving arrangements with relatives, especially older relatives. Do this well before Christmas.

3. THINK LOCAL

We all spend lots of time, energy and money in big shopping centres during the pre-Christmas run up. You can shop at your local supermarket, discount chemist, hardware or newsagent and actually spend less time and money. This is particularly the case for last-minute Christmas shopping, when just getting in and out of the shopping-centre carpark can take half an hour. We often need large shopping centres for children's gifts (those are the ones you should try to buy before December and, let's face it, you've usually been given the list well before then). Buy some good-quality generic gifts when you are doing your mid-year sale shopping (soaps, books, writing paper) ready for Christmas.

WAYS TO YOUR CHILD'S HEART AND MIND

1. Tell your child you love him or her often. It's not enough to feel it: you have to also say it regularly, through the good times and the frustrating times.
2. Maintain family rituals that demonstrate that love – bedtime reading, eating meals together, telling jokes, playing board games.
3. Treasure childhood while it lasts. Life with school-age children can be very task-orientated, but don't forget to simply enjoy the ride – it's a fast one.

FUEL

MEALS IN LESS THAN 15 MINUTES

At the end of a day's work we don't want to spend a lot of time in the kitchen, but takeaway isn't always the best solution. It's expensive and not as nutritious as something you make yourself.

1. SOY AND OREGANO LAMB CUTLETS, COLESLAW WITH YOGHURT DRESSING AND NEW POTATOES WITH MINT

Put lamb cutlets into a dish, sprinkle both sides with dried oregano and pour over some soy sauce – this combination of flavours works really well and a few minutes marinating is all that is needed. Make a dressing of half yoghurt and half mayonnaise and mix it through some packaged coleslaw (sold in the fruit and veg sections of major supermarkets – it gives good variety without all the bother of chopping). Heat a pan (preferably a corrugated cast iron chargrill pan, otherwise a non-stick pan with a little oil), and cook the cutlets for two or three minutes each side, depending on whether you want pink or well-done. Wash some new potatoes and put in a microwave dish with a sprig of fresh mint and a small amount of water. Microwave for three minutes or until nearly done. Drain and return to microwave dish with a little butter and cook for another minute. Serve.

2. PANFRIED TAIL FILLET OF SALMON OR OCEAN TROUT WITH BASIL, BROCCOLINI AND CARROT STRAWS

Tail fillets of fish are good because they have no bones. Put some plain flour (or besan – chickpea flour – gives a crisp result and a slightly different flavour) into a plastic bag, add the fish and shake to coat with flour. Heat a pan with a small amount of oil. Peel carrots and cut into straws. Trim broccolini. Remove leaves from some stalks of basil. Put the fish into the pan, skin-side down, over medium heat. Turn the fish when the skin is crisp and lower the heat to cook the other side. At this point, throw the basil leaves into the pan. While the fish is finishing, place the vegetables into a microwave dish with a little water and microwave for two minutes. Drain off the water, add some butter and cook for another minute. Serve the fish scattered with the basil leaves, which will have crisped up nicely, and the vegetables on the side.

3. GRILLED CHICKEN KEBABS WITH COUSCOUS

Chicken breast fillets work well for this. To make it really simple you can buy them ready-marinated at the butcher or chicken shop. Otherwise, cut chicken fillet into rough cubes of about 2 centimetres, and thread onto skewers, alternating with squares of capsicum and onion, if you like. Drizzle with some honey and/or soy sauce. Grill for about ten minutes, turning to cook on all sides. While the chicken is cooking, prepare the couscous according to packet directions. Sauté some pine nuts in a pan to release their aroma, then stir them through the couscous with some currants. Serve the kebabs with the couscous and some Lebanese bread. Of course, the chicken kebabs can also be barbecued, but when time is of the essence, grilling works well.

VEGETARIAN MEALS IN LESS THAN 15 MINUTES

1. HALOUMI CHEESE WITH LEMON, TOMATO AND BASIL, AND A GREEN SALAD

Make sure your haloumi cheese is from Cyprus as others tend to be tough and rubbery. You will need three slices about 1-centimetre thick per person. Put some plain flour and sesame seeds into a plastic bag, add the slices of haloumi and shake to coat. Heat a small amount of oil in a non-stick pan and fry the haloumi slices for about two minutes each side until golden brown. Serve immediately with lemon wedges, some tomato and basil tossed with virgin olive oil, and a salad of green leaves with vinaigrette (two-thirds virgin olive oil to one third wine vinegar, a dash of mustard and a pinch of salt).

2. CORN FRITTERS WITH MINTED CUCUMBER YOGHURT AND SWEET CHILLI SAUCE

Heat a frying pan with a thin slick of oil. Place one cup of self-raising flour into a bowl, crack an egg into the flour and mix with a fork. Drain a 310-gram can of corn kernels (or use creamed corn) and add to the mixture with some chopped parsley. Add about two tablespoons yoghurt or about half a cup buttermilk to thin the mixture enough so that when you put spoonfuls into the hot pan, it will spread a little to make fritters about 1-centimetre thick. As bubbles form on the surface of each fritter, turn to cook the other side. While the fritters cook, peel and finely chop a Lebanese cucumber and mix with about three-quarters of a cup of yoghurt and some chopped mint. Put the fritters onto some kitchen paper before transferring to plates and serving with a dollop of the yoghurt and some sweet chilli sauce. Serves two.

3. SPANISH OMELETTE WITH CRISP LEBANESE BREAD TOASTS

Per person you will need half a tomato, about a quarter of a capsicum, one medium seeded chilli, two eggs and some parmesan cheese, if desired. Cut two or three rounds of Lebanese bread into quarters and place on a tray in a 200°C oven. Heat a small amount of oil in a pan, chop the tomato, capsicum and chilli, and add to the pan. Cook, stirring frequently, for about five minutes or until the vegetables are well cooked down. Meanwhile, whisk the eggs lightly. Pour the eggs into the pan over the vegetables and sprinkle in a little parmesan, if you like, and a grind of pepper. When the eggs start to set, flip one side over the other. Continue to cook briefly until the omelette is barely set – don't overcook. Take the Lebanese toasts out of the oven and serve with the omelette. It's best to cook omelettes individually, or for two at the most. Keep leftover Lebanese toasts in an airtight container – they are excellent to serve with dips or soup.

WHEN YOU HAVEN'T SHOPPED

1. A PACKET OF PASTA IN THE PANTRY IS A GREAT STAND-BY

It's good simply served with some chopped garlic fried gently in butter. If you have a few anchovies and/or some parmesan, they make a great addition. And, of course, pasta with a bottled tomato sauce and some grated cheese is hard to beat when you want a quick meal.

2. A TIN OF TUNA CAN BE MADE INTO DELICIOUS FISHCAKES

Drain and mix with some leftover cooked rice or mashed potato, a finely chopped onion, an egg and a few sprigs of finely chopped parsley or any other herb you have on hand. Make into patties and shallow-fry in a little oil.

3. YOU DON'T NEED MANY INGREDIENTS TO MAKE A TASTY RISOTTO

Heat about 100 grams of butter in a saucepan and add some finely chopped vegetable, whatever you have on hand – celery, mushroom, pumpkin, broccoli and onion are all excellent. While the vegetable is cooking down, heat a litre of stock in another saucepan. When the vegetable has softened, add a cup of arborio rice and stir to coat with the butter and vegetable. Gradually add hot stock by the ladle, stirring until each addition is almost absorbed – there should still be a veil of liquid over the rice when you add the next ladleful. The risotto will take about 20 minutes to cook. Season with salt and black pepper to taste, and some parmesan is a good addition stirred in at the end. Serves two.

DIVINE DESSERTS

1. APRICOT CAKE

This divinely light cake, served warm with some lightly whipped cream, makes a delicious dessert.

800g apricots (canned halves can be substituted)
250g butter
1 cup caster sugar
4 eggs

2 cups self-raising flour, sifted
1 cup milk
ground cinnamon

Preheat oven to 180°C (170°C fan-forced). Grease and line a 24-centimetre springform cake tin. If using fresh apricots, cut in half and remove stone; if using canned, drain. Cream butter and sugar in a food processor (or use electric mixer) until light and fluffy. Add eggs, one at a time, beating well after each addition. Add the flour, mix, and continue mixing while adding the milk. Pour the mixture into the cake tin. Top with apricot halves, cut-side down – they should cover the surface. Sprinkle with cinnamon. Bake for 55 to 60 minutes or until a skewer inserted in the middle comes out clean. Serves eight.

2. LIME SEMIFREDDO WITH LIME SYRUP

½ cup caster sugar
grated rind of 2 limes
⅓ cup lime juice
4 egg yolks
1 cup cream

Simmer the sugar, lime rind and juice in a saucepan over medium heat for ten minutes or until it becomes syrupy. Meanwhile, use an electric mixer to beat the egg yolks for six minutes until light and creamy. Continue beating while adding the hot syrup and keep beating until the mixture is cool. In a separate bowl, whip the cream until soft peaks form, then fold it into the egg mixture. Pour the mixture into four 150-millilitre dariole moulds. Cover each with plastic wrap and freeze for at least four hours.

To make the lime syrup, put one cup caster sugar, the grated rind of two limes and two-thirds of a cup of lime juice into a saucepan and simmer over medium heat for about ten minutes until syrupy. Cool.

To serve, dip the moulds in warm water for a few seconds, then turn out onto plates. Pour over some syrup. Serves four.

3. CHOCOLATE AND GINGER TORTE

This cake is based on a recipe by renowned cookbook author Gretta Anna.

6 egg whites
350g caster sugar
200g coarsely chopped dark chocolate
75g mixed chopped peel
200g chopped blanched almonds
75g chopped crystallised ginger

Preheat the oven to 170°C (slightly lower if fan-forced). Grease and line a 24-centimetre springform tin. Beat the egg whites until stiff then continue beating while gradually adding the sugar. Fold in the other ingredients. Pour into the tin and bake for approximately one hour. The torte will fall slightly when taken from the oven, but don't worry about that. Whip a 300-millilitre carton of cream and spread over the top of the torte. Serves eight.

WAYS TO GROW YOUR OWN

Most herbs and aromatic leaves, such as kaffir lime and bay leaves, are better fresh, but you can end up paying a lot for a miserable amount, especially for some of the scarcer herbs. It's great to be able to pick exactly what you want when you need it and save money.

1. HERBS

Herbs are easy to grow in pots or in the garden, if you have space. They don't have to be planted in one patch; in fact it can make your garden more interesting to mix them with other plants, for instance, along a path so the fragrance is released when you brush past.

Most herbs need sun, but it doesn't have to be full sun — morning sun is fine for the majority. Basil, parsley and mint are three of the most useful, closely followed by rosemary and sage. Chives, either onion or garlic flavoured, are another basic that it's best to pick as needed as they don't store well. Onion chives are lovely in scrambled eggs, omelettes and mashed potato. Garlic chives are used a lot in Asian cooking.

Coriander is less satisfactory to grow because it quickly goes to seed and dies off, but if you stagger plantings you can keep up a supply (see recipe for 'Split pea and coriander soup' on page 240).

Chervil is a lovely herb that can be hard to find in shops, so it's an excellent one to have in your garden. It grows well in shade and has a delicate, slightly aniseed flavour that goes well in egg dishes. In *The Cook's Companion* Stephanie Alexander recommends it for scattering over cold cream soups such as green pea, cucumber or potato and leek.

Tarragon is another herb that is good to have in the garden because you can't always find it in shops, but it must be French tarragon. Russian tarragon has a nasty flavour utterly unlike the distinctive flavour of French tarragon, but unfortunately some nurseries try to pass it off as such by failing to specify the type. Pinch off a leaf and do a taste test; if a tarragon plant is on the large size and growing vigorously, chances are it's Russian — and if the label just says 'tarragon' then it's almost certainly not French tarragon. French tarragon needs plenty of sun to do well.

Both rosemary and sage require a fair amount of sun, and as rosemary is slow-growing it's best to start with an advanced plant, although it can be struck from cuttings. Rosemary and sage are hard to beat with pork, and rosemary, of course, is traditional with lamb.

Mint grows well in semi-shade as long as it gets plenty of water. Its uses go far beyond peas and new potatoes: add leaves to cucumber and yoghurt salads and it's particularly delicious with a salad of watermelon and purple onion rings.

Purple basil has a long season from spring through autumn as long as you keep cutting off the flower heads, which are a pretty addition to all sorts of salads and pasta dishes. Make pesto from either green or purple basil and freeze, so that you have that taste of summer all through winter. Here's how:

> Put two well-packed cups of basil leaves into a food processor, add 100 grams of toasted pine nuts or walnuts, 3 cloves of garlic, 120 grams of good-quality grated parmesan cheese and a cup of olive oil and process, stopping to scrape down the sides. Store in a screw-top jar or plastic container adding a film of oil over the top to keep fresh.

These quantities aren't set in stone; you can tweak them to suit yourself. When serving with pasta you can add a little of the pasta cooking water to the pesto before stirring it through the hot pasta, or after draining the pasta pour a little cream into the pot and warm before adding the pesto and stirring the pasta through. A spoon of pesto is a tasty addition to grilled or barbecued chicken and can also be stirred through savoury muffins or frittatas.

2. AROMATIC-LEAVED SHRUBS

Kaffir lime and bay trees are both great tub shrubs. It's wonderful to have fragrant kaffir lime leaves available at anytime; their use extends far beyond Thai cooking, in fact they can be used almost any time a citrus flavour is desired. The only proviso is that they are very tough so are generally discarded after they have imparted flavour — just crush them in your hands before adding to a dish — but if used as an integral part of a recipe the leaf must be cut away from the central vein and very finely chopped. Kaffir limes need full sun to fruit but as the leaves, not the fruit, are the focus, you can grow in a spot that doesn't get a lot of sun. Once it gets a start your kaffir lime will take off, competing with other shrubs for sunlight. Beware of its thorns, though — they are vicious. (See the lamb recipe that follows and 'Roast chicken with kaffir lime and sage seasoning' on page 210.)

Fresh bay leaves are so much better than dried. You won't use a lot — generally one leaf at a time is enough — but the trees can be contained well in a pot and will grow in semi-shade or sun. Bay leaves are a traditional part of a bouquet garni for flavouring casseroles and soups, and are also traditionally thrown in the pot along with peppercorns, juniper berries and cloves when cooking corned beef or pickled pork. If you make an onion sauce to go with these, a bay leaf is a good addition, and it's also used in bread sauce, the classic English accompaniment to roast chicken. Getting away from traditional uses, bay leaves can work a treat in some beef curries. Always use whole and discard when the dish is served.

SLOW-COOKED LAMB SHOULDER WITH KAFFIR LIME LEAVES

1 lamb shoulder
about 10 kaffir lime leaves
6 cloves garlic, unpeeled
about 12 anchovy-stuffed green olives
1 lemon, cut into thin slices and deseeded
olive oil

Preheat oven to 200°C. Pour a little oil into a baking dish that will just fit the lamb. Put the lamb into the baking dish on a bed of kaffir lime leaves which you have crushed lightly in your hand to release the fragrance, tucking the garlic cloves and olives under the lamb with the kaffir lime leaves. Layer the lemon slices over the lamb and drizzle a little olive oil on top. Wet a sheet of baking paper and use it to cover the lamb, tucking in loosely at the sides. Take a sheet of foil and use it to tightly seal the baking dish; repeat with a second sheet of foil. Bake for half an hour, then lower heat to 170°C and continue cooking for another three hours. The lamb should be falling off the bone. Serve with some of the lemon slices, garlic and olives. Serves three.

3. GARLIC

Australian-grown garlic is very expensive compared with garlic imported from China, but the local product has a more subtle flavour and comes in different varieties. The good news is that it's easy to grow your own garlic at virtually no cost. Many nurseries are now stocking cloves of Australian organic garlic for planting, or you can buy some good Australian garlic and save some for growing. But be warned: some garlic bought for eating has been chemically treated so it can't reproduce in gardens.

Like all bulbs, garlic grows well both in pots or in a garden bed. Plant cloves 5 centimetres deep and about 10 centimetres apart. If there is a shoot, plant so that it is just emerging from the ground. Very soon grassy shoots will appear and grow tall in no time; these can also be used as a flavouring – in garlic mashed potato, for instance – but don't harvest too many or you will rob the plant of the energy to produce a head of garlic. Garlic is ready when the leaves yellow and start to die down. Plant in autumn and harvest in summer. Freshly harvested garlic is a special treat – juicy and crunchy with a mild flavour, it is a revelation if you have never eaten it before.

To store, garlic should be dried out in a cool, dry, airy place or you can leave the stems attached, plait together and hang. If you want to get into special varieties you can order through www.garlicfarmsales.com.au. Growing garlic is a fun way to get children gardening: www.global-garden.com.au has a section called 'Growing kids' with lots of information on plants, including garlic, for children to grow.

Aioli is a wonderful garlic mayonnaise that goes brilliantly with crudités or seafood. It can be made easily in a food processor, but if you have time to spare you can make it with a mortar and pestle. This gives a better consistency, but if time is a luxury stick with the food processor version.

AIOLI

2 egg yolks
1 teaspoon French mustard
salt
1 teaspoon white wine vinegar or lemon juice
1 cup olive oil (or, for a lighter taste, ½ cup olive and ½ cup peanut or safflower oil)
8 cloves garlic (more or less as desired)
extra tablespoon vinegar

Put the egg yolks in a food processor with the mustard, salt and teaspoon of vinegar or lemon juice and process to combine. Continue processing and, using a teaspoon, trickle oil down the side of the food tube. When about half the oil has been added you can speed up the process, pouring the oil in a thin stream. At this stage you have a basic mayonnaise. Put the garlic cloves into a small microwave container with the extra vinegar and heat for 30 seconds or a minute. Add to the food processor and pulse to combine. If desired you can add a few anchovies to your aioli. Store in an airtight container in the fridge for up to a week.

Note: Heating the garlic with the vinegar prevents the sharp tang you get when you add raw garlic to mayonnaise in a food processor. The garlic has a more mellow flavour and the hot vinegar makes the mayonnaise lighter and keep better.

To make using a mortar and pestle: Crush about eight cloves of garlic with some salt, add two egg yolks, a squeeze of lemon juice and a teaspoon of French mustard, and keep working to combine, then start adding a cup of olive oil (or a blend, as above) drop by drop, mixing all the time. When you have added half the oil you can then start adding the rest of the oil in a thin stream.

CHOCOLATE TREATS TO MAKE AT HOME

1. SCRUMPTIOUS CHOCOLATE CAKE

Elizabeth David was one of the first to popularise the flourless chocolate cake. Hazelnut meal or almond meal can be used instead of flour, but the hazelnut version is particularly delicious.

250g dark chocolate
200g butter
1 tablespoon rum or whisky
6 eggs, separated
1 cup caster sugar
1 cup hazelnut meal
cocoa powder, to dust

Preheat oven to 190°C. Grease and line a 23-centimetre springform cake tin. Melt the chocolate and butter in a bowl over a pan of simmering water. Add the rum or whisky. Set aside to cool slightly. Whisk egg whites until stiff, then set aside. In a separate bowl, whisk the egg yolks and sugar until thick. Add the chocolate mixture and mix until smooth. Fold in the hazelnut meal then 1 large tablespoon of the egg white to lighten the mixture. Fold in the remaining egg white, pour into the pan and bake for 30 minutes – it will still have a slight wobble. Set aside in the pan to cool. To serve, remove the collar and turn out the cake onto a serving plate. Sift cocoa powder over the top to dust, then serve.

2. HOT CHOCOLATE MADE WITH REAL CHOCOLATE

milk (full cream, skim or anything in-between)
4 squares of dark chocolate (preferably 70 percent cocoa) per cup
sugar to taste
cocoa powder, finely grated chocolate or cinnamon

Bring milk to simmering point then, over very low heat, stir in chocolate squares with a wooden spoon, lifting off the heat if the milk starts to bubble. Stir in sugar if desired and sprinkle each serve with cocoa powder, finely grated chocolate or cinnamon.

3. CHOCOLATE TRUFFLES

240g white chocolate, broken into rough pieces
50 ml cream
30g butter
200g dark chocolate (preferably 70 percent cocoa)
cocoa powder for rolling

Put the white chocolate, cream and butter in a bowl over a saucepan containing a small amount of simmering water (do not let water touch the bowl). As the chocolate starts to melt, stir gently every couple of minutes, but do not overwork. When the chocolate has melted and the mixture has blended, remove from the heat. When the mixture has cooled slightly, put it in the fridge to firm up. Line a baking tray with baking paper. When firm, use a teaspoon to scrape up a small amount of chocolate mixture and use your hands to roll into a ball about 2 centimetres in diameter. Place the ball on the tray, and repeat with the rest of the mixture – these do not have to be perfectly shaped. Put in the freezer to set.

Melt the dark chocolate in a bowl over simmering water. Set aside to cool but do not put in the fridge. When cool, take the truffles out of the freezer and roll in the melted chocolate. The dark chocolate will set quickly on the chilled truffle mixture. When you have finished coating the truffles, put some cocoa powder in a tea strainer and sprinkle over the truffles. These are best stored in an airtight container in the freezer with baking paper between the layers and taken out a few minutes before serving. Makes about 18.

If you like, vary by using dark chocolate in the filling and dark or white chocolate in the coating, but the white chocolate as coating isn't as easy to work with. If the coating is white, do not sprinkle with cocoa powder. A tablespoon of vodka or Cointreau can be added to white chocolate truffle mixture, or a tablespoon of whisky, rum or Grand Marnier added to dark chocolate mixture – but maybe not if serving to children!

GETTING OUT OF YOUR COMFORT ZONE

It's easy to get in a rut, serving the same old meals, week after week. Be adventurous and exercise your creativity. Don't just read food magazines then set them aside. Mark recipes that interest you and make sure to cut them out and paste them in scrapbooks – one for sweet and one for savoury, or go even further with books for starters, mains, desserts, and so on. Don't allow yourself to buy the next issue until you've done this; it's a great motivator.

1. RESOLVE TO TRY A NEW RECIPE EVERY WEEK

Trying new recipes for family dinners is a good way to test recipes for entertaining and to add some excitement to everyday meals.

2. TRY SOME DIFFERENT SPINS ON OLD FAVOURITES

For instance, try this version of roast chicken — the kaffir lime leaves add a wonderful flavour and fragrance.

ROAST CHICKEN WITH KAFFIR LIME AND SAGE SEASONING

6 slices bread (preferably wholegrain)
1 onion, chopped
1 cup fresh sage leaves, loosely packed
8 kaffir lime leaves
1 number–14 chicken
olive oil or butter

Preheat oven to 190°C. Process bread to make breadcrumbs then add onion and some of the sage leaves and briefly pulse. Tip into a bowl and mix with remaining sage leaves and kaffir lime leaves, which should be crushed in the hand to release their fragrance but left whole. Stuff the chicken with the mixture. Put into a greased or oiled baking dish with some of the oil or butter on top of the chicken. Cover with a sheet of dampened baking paper, tucking it around the edges of the chicken. Cook for one hour, basting occasionally, then turn up the heat to 220°C, remove the baking paper and cook for another 15 or 20 minutes until the chicken is nicely browned. Cover with foil then rest for 20 minutes. If making gravy, add a few kaffir lime leaves and any leftover stuffing to the pan. Serves four (note that the kaffir lime leaves are not eaten).

Note: If cooking one of the larger chickens now more readily available, allow 45 minutes a kilogram at 190°C then an additional 20 to 30 minutes at 220°C until the chicken is nicely browned.

3. TRY NEW INGREDIENTS

Look for vegetables you haven't tried before in your local fruit and veg, and check out Asian supermarkets. In the latter you'll find delights such as edamame beans (see page 239), and wasabi peas (to serve with drinks), which have now become a mainstream supermarket line, frozen wontons and dumplings for adding to soups, as well as many mysterious ingredients. You can always ask for advice on how to cook them.

THINGS TO ADD TO SALADS

1. CARAMELISED WALNUTS

These started appearing in restaurant salads and have spread to the home kitchen, even scoring a mention one night on *Desperate Housewives*. They are easy to make and keep well in an airtight container.

100g walnuts
¼ cup pure icing sugar, sifted
1½ cups vegetable oil

Bring some water to the boil and add the walnuts. Simmer for five minutes. Drain well, then spread on some kitchen paper and pat dry. Put the icing sugar in a plastic bag, add the walnuts and shake. Heat the oil in a deep-sided saucepan or deep-fryer. You need a spatter shield close at hand as sugar added to oil will spit. Test that it is ready to use by adding one walnut then carefully add the others in batches. Cook walnuts until golden brown. Transfer to a tray covered with kitchen paper to absorb excess oil. Cool before storing.

2. PARMESAN CROUTONS

No caesar salad is complete without these.

8 slices white bread, crusts removed, cut into smallish cubes
2 tablespoons grated parmesan cheese
1 tablespoon olive oil

Preheat the oven to 180°C. Put the bread cubes into a bowl with the parmesan cheese and toss gently. Add the oil and toss again to coat evenly. Line a baking tray with baking paper then spread the croutons over it and bake for ten minutes. Leave to cool before storing in an airtight container.

3. MARINATED FETA CHEESE

Cut Greek feta cheese into cubes, sprinkle with dried
oregano and marinate in some olive oil. Keep in the fridge in
an airtight container. Return to room temperature before use.

ANTIOXIDANT RECIPES

A healthy diet rich in antioxidants can help prevent
heart disease and cancer and slow down the effects of
ageing. Vitamin supplements, particularly vitamin E and
vitamin C, can play a part, but by far the best source of
antioxidants are vegetables and fruit, particularly
berries. We need a minimum of five serves (half a cup or
one piece of fruit or vegetable equals one serve) of
fruits and vegetables each day.

Tea is another good source of antioxidants; it was once
thought that green tea was better than black, but recent
research suggests that black, white and green teas are
equally beneficial. But tea is better taken without milk,
as a German study claims that adding it negates some of
the antioxidant benefits (the caseins in milk decrease
the concentration of the flavonoids in tea that improve
the ability of the arteries to relax and expand).

Some antioxidant-rich foods are best eaten uncooked – berries are in this category – while others, such as tomatoes and carrots, contain higher levels of antioxidants when cooked.

The best way to benefit from a wide range of antioxidants is to embrace a multi-coloured diet. Many of the foods rich in antioxidants are a deep red or purple in colour, for instance berries, cherries, plums, beetroot, the skin of eggplant, and red kidney beans. Tomatoes, watermelon and strawberries are also rich sources. The idea is to include as many colours as possible in your diet; dark green vegetables such as broccoli and Brussels sprouts, and other lighter-coloured cruciferous vegetables such as cauliflower and cabbage. Yellow/orange vegetables like carrots, kumara (orange sweet potato) and pumpkin add to the spectrum of antioxidants.

Wholegrains are rich in vitamin E and phytic acid, powerful antioxidants that can play a role in preventing cancer.

Some nuts – such as pecans, walnuts, brazil nuts and hazelnuts – are good sources, and although spices are eaten in small amounts, many are rich in antioxidants, particularly ground cloves, turmeric and ground cinnamon.

Red wine can help keep a healthy heart, mainly because of the resveratrol and quercetin in red-grape skins. These antioxidants help blood vessels remain clear. In other good news, dark chocolate also contains antioxidants. But in the case of both wine and chocolate, it's a case of less is more in terms of health benefits.

Here are Three of the Best vegetable recipes.

1. ROASTED TOMATO SOUP

1kg tomatoes
olive oil
4 cloves garlic, chopped
1 bunch basil, leaves picked
virgin olive oil
1 medium potato, peeled and diced
2 cups vegetable stock
1 teaspoon tomato paste
black pepper
pesto to serve

Preheat oven to 190°C. Cut tomatoes in half. Pour just enough olive oil onto a baking tray to coat the surface. Place the tomato halves on the baking tray, skin-side down. Add some chopped garlic and a few basil leaves to each one and drizzle with virgin olive oil. Place in the oven and cook for about an hour – the edges should be slightly blackened. While the tomatoes are roasting, put the potato and vegetable stock into a small saucepan, bring to the boil and simmer with lid on for about 15 minutes, until the potato is cooked. Stir in the tomato paste. When the tomatoes are ready, let them cool slightly on the tray, then remove some, but not all, of the skins and discard. Scrape the tomatoes, oil and juices into a food processor and puree. Add the potato and stock, and pulse briefly. You may have to process in two batches. Pour into a saucepan and leave until you are ready to serve. Reheat gently and serve with black pepper and a dollop of pesto. Serves four.

2. SMASHING ROASTED CARROTS

Carrots have a high water content, so evaporating the water by roasting at a high heat concentrates the flavour, giving an amazing result. This is a good recipe for a dinner party because you can prepare in advance and reheat.

allow 1 large carrot per person
olive oil

Preheat oven to 220°C. Peel the carrots and cut into pieces about 3 to 5 centimetres long. Put carrots into a lightly oiled baking dish and drizzle with a little more oil. Place on top shelf of the hot oven and cook for about half an hour, turning every so often until all sides are very brown. Transfer to a serving dish and use a potato masher to smash lightly to give a chunky texture.

3. ADZUKI BEAN SALAD

This is delicious with roast or barbecued chicken, or as part of a vegetarian meal.

120g adzuki (aduki) beans, soaked overnight
4 small chillies, seeds removed and chopped
1 2.5 cm piece ginger, peeled and finely chopped

1 small Spanish onion, finely chopped
1 tablespoon coconut cream
1 teaspoon fish sauce
1 bunch snake beans
1 tablespoon peanut oil
1 bunch coriander leaves, chopped
½ cup unsalted peanuts

Put the adzuki beans in a saucepan and cover with water, bring to the boil then simmer for about 45 minutes until the beans are tender. Strain and rinse with cold water. Transfer adzuki beans to a bowl and add the chillies, ginger, onion, coconut cream and fish sauce. Stir through and set aside. Trim the snake beans and chop into small pieces about 1-centimetres long. Boil some water in a saucepan and add the snake beans, bring back to the boil and simmer for about a minute. Drain and cool. Add to the adzuki beans and stir through, then add peanut oil and coriander leaves and stir through. Strain off any surplus dressing and transfer to a serving bowl. Roughly chop the peanuts and dry fry in a pan for a few minutes until their aroma starts to release. Sprinkle over the salad. Serves eight.

BERRY RECIPES FOR ANTIOXIDANTS

You can grow your own blueberries in hanging baskets, as featured on the ABC's *Gardening Australia* program – blueberries are related to azaleas so use an azalea potting mix.

1. SUMMER PUDDING

1kg fresh or frozen berries (include some strawberries, hulled and quartered, and blueberries)

1 tablespoon water

½ cup sugar

10–12 slices slightly stale white bread, crusts removed (or substitute fruit bread, crusts removed)

Put the fruit into a saucepan with water and sugar. Cover and cook gently for a few minutes until sugar has dissolved. Set aside to cool. Cut bread slices to fit a pudding basin (six-cup capacity). Line the basin with the bread, reserving a slice or two to go on top. Make sure that the basin is completely lined and that there are no spaces for juice to escape – if necessary, overlap some slices. Spoon the fruit into the centre of the basin with enough juice to soak into the bread. Reserve remaining juice for serving. Cover the top of the pudding with bread cut to fit. Cover the surface with plastic wrap, then a small plate. Put a large can on top to weigh down and refrigerate overnight. To serve, invert the pudding onto a serving plate and pour the reserved fruit juice over. Serve with thick cream, Greek-style yoghurt, or a blend of both. Serves six to eight.

2. PASTRY CASES FILLED WITH FRESH BERRIES

120g butter

½ cup caster sugar

1 egg, beaten

1 cup plain flour, sifted

1 cup self-raising flour, sifted

1 punnet fresh blueberries, 1 punnet strawberries (hulled and quartered) – this can be varied with fresh raspberries if available

Cream butter and sugar until mixture is white and fluffy. Beat in the egg then, using a wooden spoon, stir in the flours. Knead lightly then cover with plastic wrap and chill in the fridge for about half an hour. Preheat the oven to 190°C. Lightly grease two 12-capacity small tartlet trays. Roll out the pastry on a floured board and use a glass to cut rounds to fit the trays. Use a fork to prick tartlets all over. Put in the oven and check after about 5 minutes for any areas where pastry has risen – use a teaspoon to gently press down. Continue cooking for another few minutes until pastry is a pale gold (they can now be stored in an airtight container, once cool, until ready to use, or frozen). Fill with fresh berries just before serving with a dollop of thick cream or Greek-style yoghurt on top. Makes 24.

3. BLUEBERRY SAUCE

Blueberries are delicious and nutritious in breakfast pancakes that you can make in minutes, but this sauce is sublime with crepes, the thin pancakes that make a fine dessert for more special occasions.

¼ cup caster sugar
½ teaspoon ground cinnamon
3 kaffir lime leaves (optional)
2 level teaspoons cornflour
⅔ cup water
500g fresh or frozen blueberries
grated zest of 1 lemon

Place caster sugar, cinnamon and kaffir lime leaves (if using) into a saucepan. Mix the cornflour and water in a cup and add to the saucepan, then cook, stirring, over low heat until the liquid starts to thicken. Add the blueberries and stir until the liquid clears. Add the lemon zest and, if you want a more liquid consistency, add the juice of the lemon. Remove the kaffir lime leaves before serving with crepes. This sauce, made with just a tablespoon of sugar substituted for the larger amount, is good with pork chops or roasted pork loin.

HOW TO LOSE IT

There are many different ways to achieve a desired
weight target – the hard part is maintaining it.
Contestants on television's *The Biggest Loser* achieve
dramatic weight loss but, according to *Time* magazine
(11 June, 2007), most losers find it hard to maintain
losses achieved 'through calorie restriction, endless
exercise and no small amount of dehydration that
occurs behind the scenes'. When *Time* followed up
winners and runners-up, it found that in most cases
weight rebounded once the personal trainers and
television cameras departed.

It's important to recognise that keeping weight at an
acceptable level is a lifetime effort. If you lose weight
then revert to the eating habits that put it on in the first
place you will soon go back to your old weight. And
exercise is essential: it is almost impossible to maintain
weight loss without regular exercise.

Maintaining weight loss doesn't mean depriving
yourself of all treats. In fact having the occasional
indulgence is a way of keeping the motivation to eat
sensibly the rest of the time. Life on strict rations
becomes very dull indeed, so it's best to think of your
diet on a week by week rather than day by day basis. The
idea is that if you go out for dinner or entertain,

indulge yourself. But make up for it with some low-kilojoule days the rest of the week.

A food diary is a useful way of keeping track. Work out the daily kilojoule intake required to maintain your desired weight (Allan Borushek's *Pocket Calorie, Fat and Carbohydrate Counter* is a useful aid in this calculation). For instance, if your height is 165 centimetres and you have a medium frame, your desirable weight is in the range of 56 to 63 kilograms. Say you are aiming for a weight of 60 kilograms. If you are moderately active, the daily kilojoules intake to maintain that is 8316. Convert that to a weekly budget, which gives 58,212 kilojoules. To achieve your target weight sooner you might like to start with a stricter budget – for instance, an average daily allowance of 6270 kilojoules, giving a weekly budget of 43,890 kilojoules. Keep a daily record so that you know how many you have to spare for a special occasion.

The beauty of varying your kilojoule count from day to day is that your body doesn't get used to surviving on meagre rations. The best weight loss is gradual, giving your body time to adjust to a new way of eating. If you drop your kilojoule intake too dramatically your body goes into famine mode, meaning that your metabolism functions on less kilojoules, so when you go back to a higher intake – as you inevitably will – you will gain weight faster than ever. However, kick-starting weight loss with a week or so of more drastic dieting can get you motivated. See the recipes later in this section for low-kilojoule, low-carbohydrate meals. And staying away from alcohol, which is high in empty kilojoules (those with no food value), can be a big help in the early stages. Some dieters only have to cut alcohol from their diet to see significant weight loss; cutting out alcohol and sweet treats for a month gets a weight-loss program off to a really good start.

Whatever the authors of fad diets say, weight loss comes down to taking in less kilojoules and backing it up with exercise. The variety of a well-balanced diet helps keep us motivated, so no food should be forbidden, but there are some that should be avoided most of the time. Obviously fats are high in kilojoules and there are health benefits to cutting down on saturated (animal) fats as well. So consider your fat intake very carefully. Here are Three of the Best tips for losing weight.

1. EAT SLOWLY

It takes time for the message to reach the brain that we've had enough, so by eating quickly we can be way past the point where we should leave the table than if we'd been eating more slowly.

2. EAT HIGH-FIBRE

Load up your plate with lots of high-fibre, low-kilojoule foods, mainly a variety of vegetables, salad and fruit. This prolongs the eating experience and leaves us feeling satisfied. Small helpings of kilojoule-dense foods leave us feeling hungry.

3. FINISH WITH FRUIT

Finish meals with fruit to get rid of the sweet craving. We all crave variety and the flavour contrast of something sweet, which is why we can usually fit in dessert, even at the end of a heavy meal.

FOODS TO AVOID

1. REDUCE ANIMAL FATS

Saturated (animal) fats are high in kilojoules and clog the arteries, increasing the risk of heart disease. The National Heart Foundation recommends that fat should make up only 25 percent of our daily intake of kilojoules and of that saturated fats should not account for more than a third. The American Health Foundation also found that half of all female cancers and a third of cancers in men are linked to dietary fat.

2. REDUCE REFINED CARBS

Refined carbohydrates such as white bread, white (flour) pasta, cakes and sugary breakfast cereals cause blood sugar to drop, which causes fresh hunger pangs within a few hours and the consequent temptation to snack between meals.

3. AVOID FRUIT JUICES

Fruit juices, although not unhealthy in themselves, are best avoided unless you actually want to gain weight. Once fruits and vegetables are converted to juice the calorific density becomes much higher. For instance, it takes a lot of carrots to make a glass of carrot juice (at least four), but you're unlikely to eat more than one carrot (110 kJ) at a sitting. Because of the fibre content, the kilojoules in a whole carrot are used up as the body metabolises it, but the body doesn't burn nearly as much energy metabolising a glass of juice.

WAYS TO CUT DOWN ON SUGAR

In western countries we consume an average of 22 teaspoons of sugar a day, most of it hidden in other foods. For instance, one can of soft drink contains approximately ten teaspoons of sugar, so go for diet soft drinks. Study product labels for sugar content. And if you've always had a sweet tooth, it's possible to gradually change your taste.

1.

If you prefer flavoured to plain yoghurt, try mixing half and half – 120 grams plain skim-milk yoghurt contains 302 kilojoules, while the same amount of flavoured skim-milk yoghurt contains 395 kilojoules.

2.

Reduce the amount of sugar you take in coffee or tea by doing it gradually. If you normally take two teaspoons of sugar, switch to one-and-a-half, then, after a week or so, go down to one, and so on. You'll find that your tastebuds gradually adjust to the taste and soon you'll be going without.

3.

Experiment with recipes. For instance, try reducing the amount of sugar you use in homemade cakes, puddings and biscuits. Add some extra vanilla essence or other flavouring to make up the deficit.

AVOIDING DIET BREAKERS

1.

Coming home tired and hungry can be a diet breaker unless you stock your freezer with some ready-made, low-kilojoule meals.

2.

Satisfy sweet cravings by always having some fruit or frozen low-kilojoule treats on hand (check out your supermarket for low-kilojoule, ice-cream, and so on). Even a few spoonfuls of fruit-flavoured, low-fat yoghurt will satisfy your sweet craving after the evening meal.

3.

The sight of food is a powerful appetite stimulant, so don't shop for food when you're feeling hungry. Always make a shopping list and stick to it. Also, save food magazines for when you're feeling replete; they are inspirational when it comes to cooking, but can make a hungry dieter feel even hungrier.

IDEAS FOR MODIFYING RECIPES

1.

Cut down on high-kilojoule pasta by adding a low-kilojoule vegetable, such as cauliflower or broccoli, to the pot as it is cooking. For instance, any tomato-based sauce is delicious over a mixture of penne pasta and cauliflower florets.

2.

Switch to skim milk with coffee, in milkshakes and soups, and when making any white (milk-based) sauce. You won't know the difference and neither will the family, but whole milk contains approximately twice as many kilojoules as skim milk.

3.

Most of the kilojoules in an egg are in the yolk, so when you make omelettes, scrambled eggs and soufflés, use only one whole egg per person, plus extra whites.

LOW-KILOJOULE, LOW-CARB MAIN COURSES

These low-kilojoule, low-carbohydrate meals come in at 1260 kilojoules or under. Because all three contain some protein they will leave you feeling satisfied.

1. SALAD NIÇOISE

A substantial salad that is a meal in itself.

60g tin of tuna (in brine or water), drained
1 small new potato, boiled in skin
½ cup French beans, boiled 3 minutes
1 medium egg, hard-boiled, shelled and cut into quarters
1 tomato, cut into quarters and seeds removed
2 green olives
cos lettuce leaves
1 teaspoon olive oil

juice of half a lemon
salt and pepper to taste

This salad works better served on a plate rather than tossed in a bowl – if making for a larger number, arrange salad ingredients on a platter. Mix the olive oil and lemon juice with the salt and pepper and drizzle over the salad. Serves one (approximately 1260 kilojoules).

2. WILD GREENS PIE

This is based on a traditional Greek recipe which uses wild greens gathered in the countryside. It is not necessary – and a waste of kilojoules – to brush between the sheets of filo with oil for this tasty pie.

1 bunch each of rocket and English spinach (or any mix of greens
you like)
1 leek
2 teaspoons salt
200g feta cheese, cut roughly into cubes
2 eggs, lightly beaten
⅓ cup short grain rice
nutmeg and pepper to taste
4 sheets filo pastry
1 tablespoon olive oil

Pre-heat oven to 180°C. Remove large stalks from rocket and spinach, wash well, shred finely and put in a large bowl. Chop off the coarse green part of the leek, slice it lengthways almost to the root, then slice again lengthways so that the leek is divided into four, but still joined at the base. This makes it easy to now wash the leek thoroughly and slice it across into small pieces. Add to the bowl with the greens then add the salt and toss together. Tip the greens and leek into a colander and sit over a sink or bowl for 30 minutes. Press out excess liquid then return to the bowl and combine with feta, eggs, rice, nutmeg and pepper. Brush a 23-centimetre round springform tin with some of the oil then line the tin with three sheets of filo, letting it hang over the sides. Tip the mixture from the bowl into the lined tin, then fold filo from the sides over it. Fold the remaining sheet of filo to completely cover the top and press into the sides. Brush top with olive oil. Bake for about 60 minutes or until golden. Serves six (approximately 840 kilojoules a serve).

3. VIETNAMESE CHICKEN SALAD

240g chicken breast

1 piece of ginger (about 3 centimetres), thinly sliced

2 tablespoons rice vinegar or red wine vinegar

1 teaspoon sugar

half teaspoon salt

1 carrot, peeled and cut into 3cm matchsticks

4 spring onions, sliced diagonally into 3cm lengths

2 cups bean sprouts

1 Lebanese cucumber, peeled, cut in half lengthways and sliced

1 cup mint leaves, loosely packed

1 bunch coriander, leaves only

1 medium chilli, seeds removed and sliced

1 teaspoon sesame oil

1 tablespoon fish sauce
30g roasted peanuts
lime half, cut in two

Place chicken and ginger in a saucepan with just enough water to cover, bring to simmering point and cook over low heat for about 15 minutes. Leave chicken in the liquid to cool. Mix vinegar, sugar and salt and pour into a bowl with carrot and spring onions. Set aside for 15 minutes. Roughly shred chicken and put into a serving bowl with bean sprouts and cucumber, add carrot and spring onions with their liquid, then mint, coriander and chilli, and toss together. Mix sesame oil with fish sauce, pour over the salad and toss lightly. Drain off any excess dressing. Crush peanuts and scatter over the top. Serve with lime quarters. Serves two (approximately 940 kJ a serve).

Note: You can use leftover roast or barbecued chicken with skin removed instead of cooking the chicken from scratch.

LOW-KILOJOULE, LOW-CARB SOUPS

Need to lose weight fast for a special occasion, or compensate for some over-the-top indulgence? A bowl of low-fat soup, either hot or cold, can be a meal in itself or a valuable part of a meal that will leave you feeling satisfied while spending very few kilojoules.

1. EASY TOMATO SOUP

3 cups V8 juice
3 cloves garlic, finely chopped
2 medium chillies, seeds removed
2 or 3 sprigs of parsley, chopped, or a handful of basil leaves
2 teaspoons low-fat plain yoghurt (optional)

Put juice in a saucepan with garlic and chilli and bring to simmering point. Pour into two bowls and garnish with parsley or basil. Serve hot, or chill in the fridge and serve cold. Serves two (approximately 290 kJ, or 375 kJ with the yoghurt).

2. GARLIC SOUP

Apart from water, it's hard to find anything lower in kilojoules than this soup. Although it seems like a lot, the garlic becomes amazingly mellow in flavour when cooked this way.

1 whole head of garlic (about 20 cloves)
4 cups water
2 stock cubes (vegetable, chicken or beef)
handful of fresh herbs, chopped

Remove the skins from the garlic. The easiest way to do this is to separate the cloves, then whack each one sharply with a mallet or the side of a heavy knife; the skins will fall off easily. Bring the water, garlic and stock cubes to simmering point and continue to cook gently over low heat for about half an hour, until the garlic cloves are soft – try mashing one with a fork. Ladle into two bowls with a roughly equal number of whole garlic cloves in each bowl. Sprinkle with fresh herbs. Serves two (approximately 126 kJ per serve).

3. SPINACH SOUP

2 cups water
2 stock cubes (vegetable, chicken or beef)
250g packet frozen spinach
1 medium onion, chopped
1 clove garlic, chopped
1 bay leaf
2 cups skim milk
½ teaspoon nutmeg
pepper to taste

Bring the water and stock cubes to the boil, add the spinach, onion and garlic and cook for a few minutes on low heat until the spinach defrosts and softens. Puree briefly in a blender or food processor or, better still, use a hand blender in the saucepan. Return to the saucepan, add the bay leaf, stir in the skim milk, nutmeg and pepper and heat through gently. Serves two (approximately 520 kJ a serve, or makes three first-course serves of 345 kJ a serve).

LOW-CARBOHYDRATE LUNCHES

If you're going low-carb, it's important to include some non-carbohydrate protein – egg, cheese, fish, meat or milk – otherwise you will feel hungry again in a short time. There's no doubt that sandwiches make a great easy lunch, but there are other alternatives that are easy to carry (if you want to take lunch to work) and don't take a lot of time to prepare.

1.

Salad is an obvious choice, but include ingredients that will make it special: a few prawns, some asparagus, hard-boiled egg with anchovy filling, baby beetroot, a small tin of tuna or salmon, smoked trout, roast chicken, rare roast beef, olives, feta cheese, prosciutto, artichoke, grapes, avocado, roasted peppers, snow peas, bean sprouts, endive (witlof), pear, mushroom, celery, fennel, apple, orange, figs, radish, radicchio, green beans, broccoli, cauliflower, fresh herbs – there are endless possibilities apart from the usual lettuce, tomato and cucumber.

Make a dressing to suit the ingredients and keep it separate until you're ready to eat. Here are three to try:

a. Garlic vinaigrette: 1 clove of garlic, crushed with a little salt, 1 tablespoon red or white wine vinegar, 3 tablespoons virgin olive oil, black pepper – put the ingredients in a small jar and shake to combine.

b. Horseradish cream: 1 teaspoon horseradish, 2 tablespoons Greek-style yoghurt, salt, black pepper – mix together, taste and add a little more horseradish if desired. This one is particularly good with smoked trout or roast beef.

c. Asian dressing: 1 teaspoon soy sauce, 2 tablespoons peanut oil, 1 tablespoon rice vinegar (or white wine vinegar), 1 teaspoon sesame oil, a dash of fish sauce, half a teaspoon of sugar – put in a small jar and shake to combine.

2. FRITTATAS MAKE AN EXCELLENT LUNCH DISH

They keep well in the fridge for a few days, and are easy to transport. There are many possible combinations, but this Zucchini and Feta Frittata is a favourite.

3 tablespoons olive oil
4 zucchini, thinly sliced
8 eggs
salt and black pepper
120g feta cheese, diced
2 tablespoons grated parmesan

Put 2 tablespoons of the oil into a non-stick pan (approximately 20cm wide), then sauté zucchini for about 15 minutes over a low heat until golden and very soft. Transfer to a bowl and set aside to cool. Lightly beat the eggs with the salt and pepper. Wipe the pan with some kitchen paper then heat with the remaining oil. Turn the heat to medium then pour the eggs through a strainer into the pan to remove the stringy bit that connects the yolk to the white. Spoon the zucchini evenly over the eggs, then add the feta. Leave for about one minute then reduce the heat to low. Cook for about 15 minutes until the mixture is almost set. Sprinkle parmesan over the top then brown under a griller for about five minutes. Serve at room temperature. Serves four.

3. FRUIT SALAD WITH YOGHURT

This makes a healthy lunch that can be prepared in minutes if you have some berries and, say, a mango or peach on hand. Some orange or lime juice squeezed over is a nice addition, or a dash of rose syrup (try the delicious Monin range of French syrups) is wonderful with any fruit. You can use flavoured low-fat yoghurt or Greek-style plain yoghurt with a little chopped preserved ginger stirred through it. Keep the yoghurt separate until ready to serve.

LOW GI FOODS

The Glycemic Index (GI) measures the effect of carbohydrates on blood glucose levels, so it's of great importance to anyone with diabetes or who is overweight. High GI foods contain carbohydrates that break down rapidly during digestion, releasing glucose quickly into the bloodstream so that you feel hungry again quickly. These are the baddies. Low GI foods contain carbohydrates that break down slowly, releasing glucose gradually into the bloodstream. These foods leave you feeling satisfied and reduce the desire to eat more.

It's not important to know the actual number on the GI – just whether a food is low GI (55 or less), medium (56 to 69) or high (70 or more). The old simple versus complex carbohydrate categories aren't always a reliable indicator of a food's GI, for instance basmati rice is medium GI, jasmine rice high, apples are low, pineapple medium and watermelon high. Cereals vary; for instance, Rice Bubbles and any sort of wheat flakes are high GI, while anything made with raw oats, such as porridge or muesli, is low GI.

Beans, peas and lentils are low GI foods that should feature largely in any diet based on GI measures with the exception of broad beans, which are a high GI food.

Here are Three of the Best low GI foods.

7. EDAMAME

These beans (pronounced *ed-ah-mah-may*) made their first appearance here in Japanese restaurants, usually served piled up in a bowl as a starter. But with their popularity as a stylish new vegetable, edamame beans have started popping up everywhere. They have been a staple in Asia for centuries (first recorded use in 200 BC), but in western countries their main use was in meat substitutes for vegetarians. Edamame are soybeans (a low GI food), in quite a different form to the canned and dried product that is so familiar to us. They are green, immature soybeans, picked before they ripen, and look a bit like a slightly hairy pea. Shelled they look similar to a twice-peeled broad bean, only smaller. The pods are boiled in water and sprinkled with salt, then left to cool slightly. The pod is squeezed gently and the beans popped straight in the mouth. The pod itself is never eaten.

The easiest way to buy them is in the freezer chest at Asian supermarkets, although they are starting to appear in some mainstream supermarkets as well. Frozen edamame beans are already cooked and salted and can simply be defrosted and eaten cold, but they are better put frozen into a microwave with a little water and some more salt, if desired, and warmed through. Or you can sauté them in a pan with a little water, butter or oil. These make a great healthy snack to serve with drinks. But there are as many other uses as there are for more mundane beans and peas. Shelled they can be used in salads and stir-fries, tossed with pasta, added to risotto, omelettes and frittatas … the possibilities are endless!

2. SPLIT PEAS MAKE A GREAT HEALTHY SOUP FLAVOURED WITH GINGER AND CORIANDER

SPLIT PEA AND CORIANDER SOUP

250g split green peas, soaked in water for a few hours and drained
2 tablespoons vegetable oil
1 3 cm-long knob ginger, peeled and chopped
1 bunch coriander, chopped including the roots
5 cups water
yoghurt
extra sprigs of coriander for serving

Heat oil in a saucepan with ginger and cook over low heat for five minutes. Add coriander, stir, then add split peas and stir through for a minute or so. Add the water and cook for about 30 minutes until the split peas are soft. Puree in a blender or food processor. Pour into bowls and serve with a dollop of yoghurt and a sprig of coriander. Serves three.

3. LENTILS MAKE DELICIOUS SOUPS AS WELL AS BEING THE MAIN INGREDIENT IN THE INDIAN STAPLE DHAL

LENTIL SOUP

1 cup brown lentils
2 tablespoons olive oil

1 stalk celery with leaves on, sliced
1 onion, chopped
1 carrot, peeled and diced
4 cloves garlic, chopped
2 stock cubes (vegetable, chicken or beef)
5 cups water
400g tinned chopped tomatoes
2 tablespoons tomato paste
1 small chilli, seeded and chopped
     (or leave seeds in for a hotter result
½ teaspoon cumin
1 bay leaf
½ teaspoon salt
freshly ground black pepper
fresh coriander leaves, chopped
lemon quarters and yoghurt for serving

Put lentils into a pan and cover with water, bring to the boil and drain. Set lentils aside. Put oil in the pan and cook the celery, onion, carrot and garlic until onion softens. Stir in the stock cubes, then add the water, lentils, chopped tomatoes, tomato paste, chilli, cumin, bay leaf, salt and pepper. Bring to simmering point and cook gently over low heat for about 30 minutes or until lentils are soft. Remove bay leaf. Roughly puree in a food processor or blender – the soup should be slightly chunky. Reheat with the coriander leaves. Serve with a dollop of yoghurt and squeeze in some lemon juice. Serves three.

READING FOOD LABELS

There's a lot of important information on food labels
and it's worthwhile becoming familiar with the more
important points, particularly if you're trying to lose
weight, sticking to a diet for health reasons, or suffer
from an allergy.

1.

Don't just read the energy (kilojoule/calorie) content.
It's important to check out the sugar, fat, salt and fibre
content and understand what they mean. According to
dietician Cate Lombard of The Jean Hailes Foundation
for Women's Health in Melbourne:

- sugar: 10 grams per 100 grams is a lot; 2 grams per
  100 grams is a small amount
- salt: 500 milligrams per 100 grams is a lot; 100
  milligrams per 100 grams is a small amount
- fat: 20 grams per 100 grams is a lot; 3 grams per 100
  grams is a small amount
- fibre: 10 grams per 100 grams is a lot; 2 grams per
  100 grams is a small amount.

2.

Food ingredients are listed in order of amount, so that the main ingredients are listed first and any additives (which, if present, are always in small amounts) are at the end.

Additives are listed according to their functional or class names followed by a code number, which enables you to check out the specific additive on the Food Standards Australia New Zealand website (www.foodstandards .gov.au/foodmatters/foodadditives.cfm).

These are the class names and their functions:

- *colourings* add or restore colour to foods
- *colour retention agents* retain or intensify the colour of a food
- *preservatives* help protect against deterioration caused by micro-organisms
- *artificial sweeteners* give a sweet taste for fewer kilojoules than sugar
- *flavour enhancers* improve the flavour and/or aroma of food
- *flavourings* restore taste lost due to processing, maintain uniformity and make food more palatable
- *anti-caking agents* keep powdered products, such as salt, flowing freely when poured
- *emulsifiers* help to prevent oil and water mixtures separating into layers

- *food acids* help maintain a constant level of sourness in food
- *humectants* prevent foods such as dried fruits or bread from drying out
- *mineral salts* improve the texture of foods, such as processed meats
- *thickeners and vegetable gums* improve texture and maintain uniform consistency
- *stabilisers* maintain the uniform dispersion of substances in a food
- *flour treatment agents* are substances added to flour to improve baking quality or appearance
- *glazing agents* impart a shiny appearance or provide a protective coating to food
- *propellants* are gases which help propel food from a container.

All of the additives in these categories have a number. For example, if you see 'flavour enhancer (621)' in a list of ingredients, you can identify the actual flavour enhancer as MSG (monosodium glutamate). Food colours have code numbers in the 100 range and preservatives in the 200 range. It's been claimed that a combination of some colours (102, 104, 110, 122, 124 and 129) and the preservative sodium benzoate (211) can affect children's behaviour.

3.

Other information you might see on food labels also needs to be understood:

- '97 percent fat-free' means 3 percent fat, or 3 grams in each 100 grams
- 'cholesterol-free' – can still be high in fat, but not saturated fat
- 'light' or 'lite' can mean a variety of things: light taste (as with olive oil), lightly salted, less fat – check the label carefully
- 'reduced salt' means 25 percent less salt than other foods of the same type
- 'cooked in vegetable oil' can mean palm oil, which is high in saturated fat
- 'Genetically Modified' food must be indicated
- 'best before' means food is better eaten by the given date, but is not necessarily unsafe to eat after that date. For instance, dried herbs and spices are safe to eat after the best before date, but the flavour may have deteriorated
- 'use by' means food should not be consumed after the given date for health and safety reasons
- bread can be labelled 'baked on' a certain date if its shelf life is less than seven days, which is usually the case
- if nuts are or may be present in traces, this must be indicated because of the danger of allergies
- the Glycemic Index Symbol Program started in 2002.

To be licensed to carry the GI symbol followed by a value of low, medium or high, food must meet certain nutritional criteria ensuring they contain a minimum of 10 grams of carbohydrate per serve and are not high in fat or sodium. The idea is to allow consumers to make informed choices, not necessarily excluding healthy high GI foods, but providing the best choices in different categories, such as bread, rice or breakfast cereal.

Note: At present there is little information on labels to inform consumers whether animals were treated ethically in production. When it comes to eggs produced in Australia there's no legal definition of what the term 'free-range' actually means. According to a Choice investigation three big producers account for more than half the eggs sold as 'free-range' in Australia and these eggs are produced on a truly industrial scale. Unless eggs come from an Accredited Free-Range Farm or are endorsed as 'free-range' by the RSPCA, go for 'barn-laid' endorsed by the RSPCA, or better still, organic. Be aware too that cartons of eggs are often misleadingly labelled 'farm fresh', 'all natural', 'barn-raised' and so on. President of the Australian Law Reform Commission, David Weisbrot, believes that change is needed in this area to enable consumers to make a clear choice.

THREE OF THE BEST ON IDENTIFYING
FOOD ADDITIVES

These are the chemicals that are added to your foods to give flavour, colour or a longer shelf life.

1. Flavour enhancer – MSG or monosodium glutamate – 621.

2. Colouring – 102, 2G107, FCF110, 120.

3. Preservatives: Benzoates – 210, 211, 212, 213.
   Nitrates – 249, 250, 251, 252.
   Sulphites – 220, 221, 222, 223, 224, 225, 228.

SURVIVAL

DISCLAIMER

The authors acknowledge the invaluable information provided by St John Ambulance Australia in the first aid procedures described in this section.

SAFETY PHONE NUMBERS

1.

Dial 000 for emergencies when you need the police, ambulance or fire. Never use this number for any other purpose.

2.

Dial 112 on a digital mobile phone anywhere in the world for an emergency. It automatically translates into the emergency telephone number for whatever country you are in. It doesn't work on a fixed network (use 000 instead in Australia).

3.

Dial 13 11 26 for around-the-clock advice on poisoning from the Poisons Information Centre.

CALLING FOR HELP

1.

Call 000 and state what service you need: fire, ambulance or police.

2.

Stay focused on your task and, when asked, give your name, the number you are calling from and details of what has happened.

3.

Stay at the scene and assist in the best way you can. If you are the only person at the scene of an emergency, you should try to help. If there has been a drowning, for example, have a go at lifesaving support, even if you are confused about giving breaths and chest compressions (two breaths followed by thirty chest compressions); if your last St John's course is a bit hazy, you must still have a go. If there is nothing to be done until the ambulance arrives, continue to monitor your patient and give comfort, even if that is just holding a hand. If there are experienced helpers at the scene, keep out of their way. When you get home, write a file note of what happened and what you did. Sign and date the note before you file it away.

EMERGENCY ACTION PLAN

The standard emergency action plan, as devised by St John Ambulance, consists of: **D**anger, **R**esponse, **A**irway, **B**reathing and **C**PR. Whilst DRABC doesn't exactly roll off the tongue, it does give you a plan of attack when confronted with a situation that calls for first aid. Your understanding of it could save a life.

1. IS THERE DANGER?

Have a look at your emergency scene. Are there any fallen powerlines, slippery surfaces, fires, flammable materials, rising water or unstable structures? As a general rule, don't move your patient unless it is essential because of danger.

2. IS THERE A RESPONSE?

Squeeze your patient's shoulders and ask loudly, 'Are you okay?' If your patient answers and appears conscious then leave her in that position and call 000 for an ambulance. Keep a constant check on your patient's ongoing condition until help arrives.

If you don't get a response, get someone to call 000 while you start on assessing your patient's airway and breathing.

3. IS THE AIRWAY OPEN?

Open your patient's mouth and check if there is any foreign object. If there is, put your patient on her side in the recovery position (see 'The recovery position' on page 257) and remove the object.

Once the mouth is clear, put your patient on her back and place one hand on her forehead and the fingertips of your other hand under her chin. Gently tilt back the head and lift the chin to open the airway.

Once you have opened the airway, check if there is normal breathing.

- Is the chest rising?
- Can you hear normal breathing?
- Can you feel her breath against your cheek?

If there is normal breathing, roll your patient onto her side into the recovery position.

If there is no normal breathing, call 000 for an ambulance and start rescue breaths (see 'Big three of survival' on page 255).

BIG THREE OF SURVIVAL

Once you have assessed the danger, checked for signs of consciousness, cleared the airway and determined that normal breathing is not happening, this is what should happen next.

1. BREATHING

Your patient should be on his back. If you are in doubt as to whether your patient is breathing (see previous) treat as if he isn't. The patient's forehead is tilted back and the chin is lifted. Pinch the nose with your fingers. Blow into the mouth for one second. You should see the chest move. Give a second rescue breath.

If breathing starts, turn your patient onto his side in the recovery position. Keep a check on your patient until medical help arrives.

If your patient shows no sign of life (unconscious, not breathing and not moving), start CPR.

2. CPR

Put your hands in the centre of your patient's chest and interlock your fingers. If your patient is a baby, use only two fingers. Press down on the lower half of the breastbone thirty times.

Give two breaths. Give another thirty compressions. Keep alternating with two breaths and 30 compressions until medical help arrives or your patient shows signs of life.

3. SHOCK

Shock may not sound serious, but it is a life-threatening condition. It can be caused by loss of blood, heart attack, spinal injury and other medical emergencies. The symptoms of shock are:

- weak and rapid pulse
- rapid breathing
- nausea
- dizziness.

If you suspect shock, follow DRABC (see 'Emergency action plan' on page 253) and call 000 for an ambulance.

Put your patient's legs higher than the level of his heart (unless you are dealing with a snake bite). Put your patient on their side in the recovery position if unconscious, vomiting or there are breathing difficulties.

Loosen any pressure points of clothing, maintain his body warmth and keep up an ongoing check that your patient is breathing normally.

THE RECOVERY POSITION

If your patient is on his back but you want to put him in
the recovery position to keep his airway open or remove
a foreign object from his mouth, proceed as follows.

1.

Empty the patient's pockets of hard objects, such as
keys, and kneel beside him.

2.

Move your patient's arm that is closest to you across his
chest. Put the arm that is furthest away from you straight
out on the ground so that it is at a right angle to his
body.

3.

Bend your patient's closest leg at the knee. The other
leg is straight. Roll your patient gently away from you
onto their side. Support the head and neck.

BEING PREPARED

1. THE FIRST AID KIT

You can buy first aid kits from the chemist, supermarket or online. Better still, call St John Ambulance Australia on 1300 360 455 or Australian Red Cross on 1300 367 428. Put a kit in your house and one in your car. The contents need to be in a childproof plastic box. To make your own you will need a small selection of:

- sterile cotton gauze swabs for cleaning wounds
- hand towels for general cleaning
- bandaids in different sizes for small cuts
- a roll of adhesive strapping to hold dressings in place
- sterile, non-adhesive dry dressings for burns and wounds
- sterile wound dressings for eye pads or bleeding
- rolls of stretch bandage for poisonous bites
- triangular calico bandages for splints and slings
- large safety pins for holding bandages
- a small pair of scissors
- a pair of tweezers for removing stings and splinters
- sealable plastic bags for carrying water and making icepacks
- disposable gloves
- an approved resuscitation mask for infection control

- pencil and notepaper for record-making and messages
- individually wrapped alcohol swabs for cleaning around wounds
- a sterile combined dressing for covering wounds
- one plastic bottle of saline solution for cleaning eyes, wounds and burns
- one sting relief treatment
- a first aid book (also available from St John Ambulance Australia or Australian Red Cross)
- aspirin.

2. DO A FIRST AID COURSE

The very best action you can take to be prepared is to complete a first-aid course. You can contact St John Ambulance Australia on 1300 360 455 or www.stjohn .org.au, or Australian Red Cross on 1300 367 428 or www.redcross.org.au for details.

3. HOME SAFETY SCREENING

Undertake a safety check of your house, garage and garden by looking for some obvious and hidden dangers. Once you have surveyed the scene as an adult, get down on your knees and imagine you are a child.

FIRST AID FOR BABIES AND TODDLERS

1. FEBRILE CONVULSIONS

Convulsions occur when a child has a high temperature.

SIGNS

- fever
- twitching of face or limbs
- eyes rolling back
- blue face or lips
- stiff or floppy body
- convulsions
- difficulty breathing
- can become unconscious

ACTION

- Put your patient on the floor and protect him from harm. Do not try to restrain him.
- Assess your patient's breathing. If not breathing, start CPR (see 'Big three of survival' on page 255) and call 000 for an ambulance.

PREVENTION

- Remove excess clothing from an unwell child
- Keep temperature under control with cool water sponging and medication if advised.

2. CROUP AND EPIGLOTTITIS

Croup is a viral infection of the voicebox and windpipe and usually occurs after a cold or sore throat.

SIGNS

- barking seal-like cough
- cold-like symptoms
- pale, clammy skin
- difficulty in breathing
- slight temperature
- worse symptoms at night

ACTION

- Give your patient reassurance. Croup is a distressing disease, especially with repeated attacks, but it is not serious.
- Control any fever on medical advice and keep your patient hydrated with liquids. Do not use steam to ease breathing.
- If there is severe difficulty with breathing, get medical help.

Epiglottitis is a bacterial infection of the epiglottis, which is the valve that guards the airway. Children between the ages of two and seven are most at risk. It can be life-threatening.

SIGNS

- flushed skin
- high temperature
- child is quiet – no coughing or talking
- saliva drool

- unable to swallow
- anxious
- purr-like noise when breathing out
  ACTION
- Call 000 for an ambulance.
- Keep your patient calm and support him in a comfortable position.
- Do not examine your patient's throat.

3. ANAPHYLAXIS

This is the most severe form of allergic reaction and it can be life-threatening. Known triggers include:

- nuts
- sesame seeds
- shellfish
- cow's milk
- soy
- egg
- wheat
- royal jelly
- bee stings
- wasp stings
- latex
- antibiotics.
  SIGNS
- itchy, raised rash
- swelling of throat, lips, tongue and eyes

- difficulty speaking, breathing and swallowing
- loss of consciousness or dizziness
- headache
- vomiting
- rapid, irregular pulse
  ACTION
- Call 000 for an ambulance.
- Stay with your patient, keep him calm in a lying or sitting position.
- Use an Epipen (self-administered adrenaline) if available.
- If unconscious, give CPR (see 'Big three of survival' on page 255).

Contact the Australasian Society of Clinical Immunology and Allergy (www.allergy.org.au) for more information.

FIRST AID FOR CHILDREN

1. DROWNING

Anyone can drown in a few centimetres of water. Care, particularly with children, should be taken in the bath, pool, spa, and paddling pool, or near fishponds, open drains and even buckets of water.

At a beach, lake, dam or river, do not attempt to rescue a drowning person if it is beyond your swimming capability, otherwise two people will be needing help. You could of course throw a life ring, foam esky, bodyboard or oar.

SIGNS

- decreased level of consciousness
- not breathing
- blue face
- possibly no pulse
- possibly foam from the nose or mouth

ACTION

- Dial 000 for an ambulance and follow DRABC (see 'Emergency action plan' on page 253).
- Check your patient's airway for any foreign objects or vomit and check whether breathing is regular. If not, give rescue breaths (see 'Big three of survival' on page 255). Time is of the essence so start the breaths as soon as possible, even if you are still in shallow water.
- On dry land, start CPR (see 'Big three of survival' on page 255).
- Once your patient is stable, place in a recovery position (see 'The recovery position' on page 257). Consider hypothermia and use blankets or towels to slowly raise the body temperature.

PREVENTION

- Teach your children to swim and respect water.
- Learn to swim yourself.
- Never leave children unattended in any water, no matter how shallow.
- Never leave children unattended on the beach.

- Try to always swim with a buddy.
- Ensure all pool and spa fencing conforms with Australian Standard AS 1926.
- Never leave children to mind other children in water.

Contact: the Royal Life Saving Association in each state, or the national office on (02) 8217 3111 (www.royallife saving.com.au).

2. MENINGITIS

Meningitis is the inflammation of the meninges (the membrane lining of the brain and spinal cord). It usually refers to infections caused by viruses, or bacteria.

Bacterial meningitis can be life-threatening and needs immediate medical help. Some bacteria that cause meningitis can also cause blood-poisoning, or septicaemia. There are other types of meningitis with similar symptoms but different treatments.

SIGNS (not all will appear at one time or at all) for adults and children

- stiff neck
- headaches
- fever
- vomiting
- sensitivity to light
- drowsiness
- confusion
- joint pain

- fits
- rash. This might be a pink rash, or purple, pink or red spots. It can also appear as pink, red, purple or brownish-coloured pin-prick spots that can develop into a bruise-like rash. The rash does not usually fade when pressed with a glass but this test is not always dependable.

SIGNS for infants

- fever (maybe cold hands or feet)
- refusing food
- vomiting
- high-pitched moaning
- doesn't like being handled
- neck retracted with back arching
- blank or staring expression
- difficult to wake or lethargic
- pale, blotchy complexion
- rash (see the description under 'meningitis' above)

ACTION

- Seek medical help.
- If you are dissatisfied with the diagnosis, seek further medical help. Prompt action is vital.

PREVENTION

- There are vaccines that protect against some types of meningitis. There is no vaccine that will protect against all types.

Contact the Meningitis Centre on 1800 250 223 (www.meningitis.com.au) for more information.

3. POISONING

Poisons can be inhaled, eaten or absorbed, and children are at special risk.

SIGNS
- abdominal pain
- drowsiness
- nausea
- vomiting
- burning pains from mouth to stomach
- breathing difficulties
- tight chest
- blurred vision
- odours on the breath
- change of skin colour with blueness around lips
- sudden collapse

ACTION
- If your patient is conscious, follow DRABC (see 'Emergency action plan' on page 253 and 'Big three of survival' on page 255). Wash patient's mouth and lips before starting CPR.
- Call 000 for an ambulance.
- If your patient is conscious, try to find out the type of poison and write it down or hold onto the container.
- Call 13 11 26 for the Poisons Information Centre (24 hours, 7 days).
- Do not induce vomiting unless you have been told to by medical help.

PREVENTION

· Store chemicals, cleaning products, beauty products, weed and snail killers, gardening products, baits and medicines at least 1.5 metres off the ground in their original childproof containers.

· Don't take medicine in front of children or describe them as sweets or vitamins.

· Take extra care with storing products if a child is home sick, or you are cleaning out cupboards or moving house.

· Ensure there are no poisonous plants in the garden such as oleander, angel's trumpet, rhubarb leaves and foxgloves.

Contact the Poisons Information Centre on 13 11 26 for more information or advice.

FIRST AID IN THE HOME

1. CHOKING

With a partially or completely blocked airway your patient may not be able to talk, so you need to be able to spot the signs.

SIGNS

· gagging
· clutching at throat

- coughing
- trouble speaking and breathing
- wheezing
- face, neck, lips, ears and fingernails turning blue
  ACTION for an adult or child over one year of age
- Try to get your patient to relax and breathe deeply. Encourage her to cough.
- If no improvement, bend your patient forward to give five sharp blows between the shoulderblades. Check to see if the obstruction has cleared after each blow.
- If no improvement, do five chest thrusts. Put one hand in the centre of their chest and one hand in the middle of their back for support. Check to see if the obstruction has been dislodged after each thrust. If still no success, continue with five back blows and five chest thrusts until help arrives.
- If your patient is unconscious, call 000 for an ambulance and start CPR (see 'Big three of survival' on page 255).
  ACTION for an infant under one year of age
- Call 000 for an ambulance.
- Put the infant facedown on your forearm. Support the head and shoulders with your hand. Open the mouth with your hand.
- With the base of your other hand, give five sharp blows between the shoulderblades. Check after each blow to see if the obstruction has cleared and, if it has, remove it with your fingers.

- If no success, put the infant on her back on a firm surface. Put two fingers in the centre of the chest and give five chest thrusts.
- If not cleared, alternate five back blows and five chest thrusts until help arrives.
- If your patient is unconscious, call OOO for an ambulance and start CPR (see 'Big three of survival' on page 255).

PREVENTION

- Teach your children to eat and drink slowly, chew food properly and not put objects in their mouths.
- Don't give children under five years of age nuts, hard sweets, coins or pens with caps.
- Keep curtain and blind cords very short or stored high up on hooks.

2. BURNS

ACTION

Get medical help if your patient:

- Has a burn larger than her palm.
- Has inhaled smoke or fumes.
- Is an infant or child.
- Has burned hands, face, airways or genitals
- Has a deep burn.
- Has a burn and you don't know how serious it is.

If your patient's clothing is on fire, wrap them in a rug or blanket and roll on the ground.

- Cool the burned area under cold running water, under a shower if necessary, for 20 minutes or more.
- Remove clothing or jewellery from the burned area unless they are sticking to the burn.
- Cover the area with a clean, non-stick dressing. Do not put any creams on the burn.

PREVENTION

- Install smoke alarms in your home.
- Have your hot water temperature set at 50°C.
- Ensure your heaters or fires are guarded from people, curtains and flammable material.
- Keep kettle cords short and out of reach of children.
- Keep pot handles turned to the back.
- Store away matches, cigarettes and gas lighters.
- Put a fire blanket or extinguisher in the kitchen.
- Work out a family home escape plan.

3. DOMESTIC ELECTRIC SHOCK

Electric shock from household appliances can result in burns, external or internal, or interfere with the heart.

SIGNS

- difficulty breathing or no breathing
- no pulse or weak pulse
- burns
- collapse
- unconsciousness

ACTION

- It is vital that you disconnect your patient from the source of the electricity. Do not touch your patient until you have done that. Either turn off and disconnect the power at the outlet, or push your patient away from the source with something that will not act as a conductor, such as a rug, towel or a wooden object.
- Call 000 for an ambulance. If your patient has stopped breathing, start rescue breaths (see 'Big three of survival' on page 255). If your patient's heart has stopped, commence CPR (see 'Big three of survival' on page 255).

PREVENTION

- Make sure you have a safety switch in your fuse box.
- Put safety plugs in your power points.
- Store electric hair dryers safely — don't leave them in the bathroom plugged into the power point.

Contact Energy Australia for safety tips (www.energyaustralia.com.au).

FIRST AID ON THE ROAD

1. SPINAL INJURIES

SIGNS
- loss of feeling or tingling in the hands or feet
- loss of movement in arms and legs
- pale, clammy skin
- unnatural pose
- may be an absence of pain

ACTION
- Call 000 for an ambulance. If your patient is unconscious, follow DRABC (see 'Emergency action plan' on page 253 and 'Big three of survival' on page 255).
- Do not move your patient unless necessary, for example, your patient is unconscious and requires CPR or there is a danger of fire.
- Support the neck and head at all times by placing hands on either side of head until medical help arrives.
- Apply an improvised collar (using a towel or newspaper) if help is delayed.

PREVENTION
- Always use seatbelts.
- Always use protective headgear for contact and high-speed sports.

- Always play sport safely with a good understanding of the rules.
- Never dive into any water without first checking the water depth. Never dive into any water that could have submerged rocks, timber or debris.

Contact Spinal Injuries Association (www.spinal.com.au) for more information.

2. LIFE-THREATENING BLEEDING

ACTION
- Call 000 for an ambulance.
- Lie your patient down. If necessary, remove or cut away clothing to expose the wound.
- Apply direct pressure over the wound with a pad or your hands (wear gloves if you can). If possible, push the wound edges together.
- If possible, raise the injured body part above the level of the heart.
- Secure the pad with a bandage. If bleeding is not under control, apply a second pad on top of the first one. Make sure the bandage is not too tight and recheck every 15 minutes.
- Apply a constrictive bandage as a last resort when medical help has not arrived and the situation is life-threatening.

PREVENTION

- Store razors, tools and knives safely.
- Glass doors, shower screens and low-level windows should be made with safety glass.

3. CLOSED FRACTURES

SIGNS

- pain at the site
- tenderness
- swelling
- pale, clammy skin
- loss of power

ACTION

- Call 000 for an ambulance.
- Immobilise the injury with a splint and broad bandages. If possible, use a padded splint such as a piece of wood with cloth wrapped around it or another part of the patient's body.
- Check that the bandages are not too tight and recheck every 15 minutes for swelling, pain, lack of warmth, blue skin, lack of pulse or tingling below the bandage.

PREVENTION

- Keep your driveway separated from the play area of the garden.

FIRST AID IN THE OUTDOORS

1. SNAKE AND FUNNEL-WEB SPIDER BITES

Pay particular respect to brown, tiger, taipan, black and death adder snakes. Anti-venom is available for all of these, but you should follow the action plan.

SIGNS

- puncture marks
- pale, cool skin becoming sweaty
- rapid pulse
- nausea
- vomiting
- difficulty breathing
- collapse

ACTION

- If your patient is unconscious, follow DRABC (see 'Emergency action plan' on page 253 and 'Big three of survival' on page 255).
- Call 000 and ask for an ambulance.
- Your priority is to slow the movement of the venom through your patient's body — if the patient panics and runs around for help, it could prove fatal. Get your patient to rest and be calm. Don't cut, wash or suck the bite.
- Apply pressure directly over the bite. Apply a pressure bandage starting from the bite and keep winding up the affected limb, either to the armpit or the groin.

- Apply a second bandage from the fingers or toes, depending on whether an arm or leg is affected, and again wind up as far as possible to the armpit or groin.
- Put on a splint to keep the affected limb still. Do not elevate the limb.
- If you can't do any of these steps, keep heavy pressure on the bite area and get help. For example, ask a patient with a bite on their finger to sit on their own hand while you run for help.

ACTION for non-fatal spiders

- If your patient is bitten by a red-back, white-tailed, trap-door or wolf spider, apply a cold compress for the pain and get medical help.

PREVENTION

- Keep your lawn short and stay out of long grass.
- Remove rubbish piles from the garden.
- Cover up hands and feet when you are gardening.

Contact Poisons Information Centre on 13 11 26 (24 hours, 7 days) for more information.

2. EYE INJURY

ACTION

If the injury is not serious (minor irritation):

- Wash the eye with a gentle stream of clean water or sterile saline.
- If unsuccessful, seek medical help.

If the injury is a penetrating object:

- Get your patient to lie flat.
- Call 000 for an ambulance.
- Cover the injured eye. Do not pull the penetrating object out of the eye. Unless it is necessary for safety, do not move your patient.

PREVENTION

- Wear safety glasses with side shields for jobs where flying hazards are likely, for example, lawnmowing.
- Wear eye protection for eye-danger sports, for example, squash.
- Keep garden shrubs and trees pruned above eye level.

3. HEAT EXHAUSTION

SIGNS

- clammy, pale skin
- rapid breathing
- heavy sweating
- nausea
- vomiting
- headache
- cramps

ACTION

- Get your patient to rest in the shade by lying down and removing excess clothing. Sponge down with cold water.
- If the nausea has passed, slowly sip water.

- Consider medical help if your patient is vomiting or does not recover promptly.

Heatstroke (or core temperature emergency) is a far more serious condition where the body's temperature regulation centre in the brain has been rendered inoperative and the body's temperature keeps going up.

SIGNS
- flushed, hot, dry skin
- core temperature of 40.5°C or more
- irrational or aggressive behavior
- vomiting
- collapse, seizure, coma

ACTION
- Follow DRABC (see 'Emergency action plan' on page 253 and 'Big three of survival' on page 255).
- Remove your patient's clothing and apply cold packs of ice to the neck, groin and armpits.
- Cover with a wet sheet and use a fan to cool further.
- Call 000 for an ambulance.
- If your patient is completely conscious, give water.

PREVENTION
- Avoid physical activity in the hottest part of the day.
- Keep drinking water; wear a hat and cool clothing.
- Never leave anyone in a closed car.
- Pay particular attention to people over 65, babies, young children, pregnant women, nursing mothers, and people with heart disease or high blood pressure.

FIRST AID FOR BYSTANDERS

1. EPILEPTIC SEIZURE

Epileptic seizure is a disruption of normal brain function which causes fits.

SIGNS

- sudden cry and fall to the ground
- blue face and neck
- jerky muscular movement
- froth at the mouth
- biting the tongue
- loss of bladder and bowel control

ACTION

- Follow DRABC (see 'Emergency action plan' on page 253 and 'Big three of survival' on page 255).
- Protect your patient from injury but do not restrict his movement or put anything in his mouth.
- Place your patient on his side as soon as possible. Allow your patient to sleep but continue to monitor him.
- Consider medical help if the seizure continues for more than five minutes, another seizure follows or there are injuries.

Contact Epilepsy Action Australia on 1300 374 537 (www.epilepsy.org.au) for more information.

2. FAINTING

Fainting occurs when blood supply to the brain is not sufficient. It may happen if someone has been standing still for too long, there has been a sudden change of position, there has been an injury, or there has been an unpleasant experience.

SIGNS

- giddy
- blurred vision
- weakness
- pale, clammy skin
- yawning
- temporary loss of consciousness
- slow, weak pulse

ACTION

- Lie your patient down. If conscious, raise the legs whilst keeping the head and body flat. Loosen any tight clothing.
- If unconscious, put your patient in a recovery position. If not recovering quickly, follow DRABC (see 'Emergency action plan' on page 253 and 'Big three of survival' on page 255) and get medical help.
- Check for injuries and allow your patient to rest.

3. CARDIOVASCULAR DISEASES

Cardiovascular disease is the leading cause of death in Australia, accounting for over 30 per cent of deaths in recent years. It kills one Australian every ten minutes.

Heart attack is a blockage of a heart artery when the heart muscle is damaged due to lack of oxygen. The blockage usually comes about because of a build-up of fats (in particular cholesterol).

SIGNS

- pain (mild, moderate or severe) in the centre of the chest; sudden or slow onset
- pain may spread to the neck and throat, jaws, shoulders, back or both arms
- shortness of breath
- sweating
- nausea
- vomiting
- dizziness
- collapse

ACTION

- Call 000 for an ambulance.
- If conscious, get your patient to rest, take any relevant medication or an aspirin in water.
- If unconscious, do CPR (see 'Big three of survival' on page 255) and/or use an automated external defibrillator (AED) if one is available. The AED is an electronic device which gives the patient a controlled electric shock to the heart. Turn on the AED and

attach the electrode pads. The device will give voice or visual prompts as to how to use it. Once the device has analysed the patient's heart rhythm it will either deliver the shock automatically to the patient or direct you to push the shock button. Do not touch your patient while the device is analysing the rhythm or administering the shock.

Contact the Heart Foundation on 1300 362 787 (www. heartfoundation.org.au) for further information.

Stroke happens when blood flow to the brain is interrupted either by a clot or a blood vessel rupturing, causing blood vessels to die. It can cause death or permanent damage if not treated quickly. Someone has a stroke every 45 seconds and dies as a result of one every three minutes. Three out of five victims are women. It can be tricky to pick but as time is of the essence, assume the worst.

SIGNS
- sudden and very bad headache
- sudden nausea
- sudden vomiting
- loss of balance
- loss of consciousness
- blurred vision
- loss of coordination or weakness, often on one side

ACTION

· There are three simple tests for detection. It's easy to remember them by the first three letters, **STR**:

   a. **S**mile – ask your patient to smile.

   b. **T**alk– ask your patient to say a simple sentence coherently, for example, 'Today is hot.'

   c. **R**aise – Ask your patient to raise both arms.

If your patient has trouble with any of these tasks, call 000 for an ambulance. Another possible sign is a crooked tongue. Ask your patient to stick out his tongue.

PREVENTION

· Healthy diet and regular exercise.

Contact the National Stroke Foundation on 1800 787 653 (www.strokefoundation.com.au) for more information.

SURVIVING THE SPORTING LIFE

1. ASTHMA

Brought on by a constriction of the airways, asthma causes breathing difficulties. It is often triggered by exercise as well as stress, house dust, allergens and smog. Severe attacks can lead to collapse and respiratory arrest.

SIGNS

- shortness of breath
- coughing
- chest tightness
- wheezing

ACTION

- If your patient is unconscious, call 000 for an ambulance and follow DRABC (see 'Emergency action plan' on page 253 and 'Big three of survival' on page 255).
- If your patient is conscious, help your patient to sit up and lean forward or find a comfortable position. Encourage her to take deep, slow breaths.
- If your patient has medication, give four puffs. If no improvement after four minutes, give another four puffs.
- If no improvement, call 000 for an ambulance.
- Give a child four puffs every four minutes.
- Give an adult six to eight puffs every five minutes until medical help arrives.

Contact the National Asthma Council Australia (www.nationalasthma.org.au) for more information.

PREVENTION

- Work toward medical diagnosis and appropriate medication.
- Always carry medication, particularly when exercising.
- Always have a good warm-up before exercise.

- Try to exercise in moist, warm air as opposed to cold, dry air, for example, do some laps in an indoor pool rather than go for an early morning run in winter.
- Don't exercise in dusty or mouldy environments, such as badly maintained gyms.
- Cardiovascular exercise can improve asthma.

2. SOFT TISSUE INJURY

Hopefully this will be your most common first aid duty. Use this information for bruises (bleeding into the deep tissue), sprains (stretching or tearing of the ligament) and strains (overstretching of the muscle or tendon).

SIGNS
- pain
- swelling
- tenderness

ACTION (or **R.I.C.E.D.**)
- **R**est your patient and their injury.
- **I**ce pack to the injury for 20 minutes and reapply every two hours for the first 24 hours. Then every four hours for the next 24 hours. Don't put ice directly on the skin.
- **C**ompression bandages or elastic bandages.
- **E**levate the injury.
- **D**iagnosis, meaning, early treatment will lead to a quicker recovery.

PREVENTION

· Always gently warm-up before exercise, including stretches, and again when cooling down after exercise.

3. DIABETIC EMERGENCY

Diabetes is a serious disease that is caused by blood sugar imbalance in the blood. There are two types: Type 1 occurs in young people, due to a deficiency in producing insulin; and Type 2 occurs in adults, generally due to obesity.

If you are not sure whether you are dealing with a low blood sugar or high blood sugar emergency (as described below) give a sweet drink. (Usually you are dealing with low blood sugar, often brought on by unaccustomed exercise.)

SIGNS of low blood sugar

· pale
· hungry
· sweating
· weak
· confused
· aggressive

ACTION

· If your patient is unconscious, follow DRABC (see 'Emergency action plan' on page 253 and 'Big three of survival' on page 255).

- If your patient is conscious, give sweet food or drink (not diet or sugar-free) every 15 minutes until medical help arrives.

SIGNS of high blood sugar

- thirsty
- need to urinate
- hot, dry skin
- acetone breath

ACTION

- If unconscious, follow DRABC (see 'Emergency action plan' on page 253 and 'Big three of survival' on page 255).
- If conscious, help your patient to self-administer insulin.
- Call 000 for an ambulance.
- Give sugar-free drinks if help delayed.

PREVENTION

- Type 1 diabetes usually requires regular insulin injections.
- Type 2 diabetes usually requires dietary management.
- Regular aerobic exercise can decrease insulin dependency.

Contact Diabetes Australia on 1300 136 588 (www.diabetes australia.com.au).

SURVIVING A DAY AT THE BEACH

Over 85 percent of us live within 50 kilometres of
the coast, so at some stage this Three of the Best will
come in handy.

1. BLUEBOTTLES

There is a diversity of opinion as to what is the best
remedy. Some options soothe, such as ice and sting
cream. So as to deactivate the toxins, try putting the sting
and skin in hot water (45°C and no hotter).

2. SUNBURN

You should find some shade at least for the hottest time
of the day. Go to the beach early in the morning. Invest
in caftan tops and light pants or protective swimming gear
– this is no longer fashion suicide. Wear a generous hat
and a pair of sunglasses. Use factor 30+ sunscreen that is
water resistant and reapply every couple of hours. Even if
you don't do the right thing, make sure any children you
bring to the beach are well protected. Sunburn in
childhood is a risk factor for skin cancer later in life.

You might need to change your outlook on tanning and pass it on to your children. The bottom line is that a suntan is irreversible skin damage. Don't go to a solarium as a substitute for a beach tan or to get your skin 'ready' for a sunny holiday. Exposure at a solarium, just like the beach, increases your risk of skin cancer.

3. RIPS

A strong current running out to sea is the most likely cause of getting into trouble in the surf. Rips usually look different from the water around them. Sometimes they are a darker colour, or murkier, or the water is rippled with calm water surrounding, or covered in debris. If you get stuck in one, stay calm and go with it. Float and put your arm up for help. If there is no help available, swim in a line with the shore until you reach the area where the waves are breaking and use the waves to return to the shore.

Surf Life Saving Australia can give you education and training. Contact them online at www.slsa.com.au or via the Surf Life Saving Association in your state.

HANGOVER SOOTHERS

1. Before going to bed, drink a big glass of water, or
    soda water if you feel like some fizz, and have a
    back-up supply on the bedside table with some
    paracetamol in case a headache develops.

2. In the morning, have some Vegemite toast and a
    glass of orange or tomato juice with a Berocca or
    vitamin B tablet.

3. At lunch it helps to have a substantial meal of, say,
    fish and chips or steak and chips washed down with
    a milkshake or banana smoothie.

CAR COLOURS YOU WOULDN'T BE SEEN DEAD IN

Car colours do impact on your chances of having a
collision. Silver might be a popular fashion statement
but it's not at the top of the colour safety findings. In
fact, silver cars have a 10 percent greater crash risk
than white.

Red, associated with all things safety and making cars
drive faster, is in fact one of the least visible colours on

the spectrum, especially at night or in peripheral vision. Here, for the Australian environment, are Three of the Best. If you are driving a maroon, navy, dark green, brown, grey or black car, think about putting your parkers on if the light is not bright.

1. WHITE

This is the safest colour, according to Monash University's Accident Research Centre. (Unless, of course, you are driving in snow, in which case you are better off in bright yellow or orange.) White is also the best for heat and offers good resale.

2. LIGHT

Colours such as light yellow.

3. BRIGHT

Fluorescent colours such as lime green may not be a fashion choice, but they are very safe on the road.

CAR TRICKS

1. JUMP-STARTING YOUR CAR

If your battery is nearly flat, but not dead, you can jump-start your car with a pair of jumper leads. Buy a set from a car accessory shop and keep it in your boot. Find a friendly motorist and have your cars facing nose to nose, but not touching. Both car ignitions should be off. They should be in park or neutral and the handbrakes on.

- Take the red end of the jumper lead and put it on the 'good' battery terminal. (If the terminal is not red, it should have a positive (+) on it.)
- Put the other red end of the jumper lead on your lifeless red terminal.
- Take the black end of the jumper lead and put it on the 'good' battery terminal. (If the terminal is not black, it should have a negative (−) on it.)
- Put the other black end of the jumper lead on your lifeless black terminal.
- Turn on the ignition of the 'good' battery car and let it run for a short while.
- Turn on the ignition of the lifeless battery car. Leave both cars idling for five minutes.
- Take off the black and red jumper leads while the cars are still running.

If you don't have jumper leads or a willing helper but you do have a manual car, you can roll-start it. If you are on a hill with a straight stretch of road ahead, turn the ignition on and put the car in second gear with your foot pushing in the clutch. Release the handbrake and roll down the hill. As the car gathers speed, quickly take your foot off the clutch and the car should lurch into life. Put your foot back on the clutch to prevent it stalling and let the engine idle for a few minutes. Engage first gear and drive off with satisfaction.

2. RECOVERING FROM A SKID

If there is oil, snow or ice on the road, you could find yourself in a skid. Don't try to turn the steering wheel so as to drive out of the spin. Every fibre in your body will want to do this, but in fact it is the worst evasive tactic you could make. Calmly turn the steering wheel into the direction the spin is taking the car. At the same time, slowly take the pressure off the accelerator. As the car straightens up, bring the steering wheel back to centre.

Corners are particularly treacherous in bad conditions. Focus on rolling into corners (try to avoid braking into them) and accelerating out of them.

The recovery from a skid is counter-intuitive, so if you are worried, do an advanced driving course and get a feel for it.

3. BRAKE FAILURE

It's rare and the stuff of nightmares. If you are on the flat and applying the brakes with no effect, indicate to your left and pull over. Put on your hazard lights while the car is slowing, change down gears if you are in a manual or, in an automatic, shift into low gear (first gear). Don't attempt to put the car into reverse. Try to get off the road safely. Use your horn to warn pedestrians or other cars.

If you are on a hill, follow the same steps. If you are still travelling too fast to safely leave the road, slowly pull on your handbrake. (If you do it too quickly you will lose control of the car.)

As a last resort and if all else fails, use the curb, safety fence, cement dividers or guardrails to slow the car by friction. Gravel or dirt on the shoulder of the road will slow the car, as will small bushes. The faster you are going the more dangerous these last-ditch options become.

CHANGING A TYRE

Always have a jack, wheel brace and spare wheel in the boot. You might also want to include a pair of soft gloves. It's a good idea to practice, so throw a 'spare tyre' party with a few girlfriends (but keep the alcohol on ice until after you've perfected the technique). Before you start, make sure you are on a flat, solid surface, with the hazard lights and handbrake on. Put the car in park or first gear.

1. THE JACK

Position the jack below the little row of grooves which are impressed on the under edge of the car near the wheel. Turn the handle of the jack to take a bit of the weight off the flat tyre.

2. THE BRACE

Put the wheelbrace over the wheel nuts and turn anti-clockwise to loosen. Put your foot on the brace in a horizontal position to lever for extra strength. Turn the handle of the jack again to take the car a little higher. Remove the flat tyre.

$\mathcal{3}.$ THE NEW TYRE

Put the new tyre on and tighten the wheel nuts by hand. Lower and remove the jack. Give the wheel nuts a final tighten with the brace. Pack your kit and dead tyre very securely back in the boot. Don't forget to buy a replacement spare tyre as soon as possible.

CAR SAFETY

$\mathcal{1}.$ PARKING

Women spend a lot longer than men just sitting in the car. We do the food shopping and sit in the car going through the list. We arrive for a work appointment and go through notes. Sometimes the car is a second office and control centre. It also makes you vulnerable. If you are sitting in the car, always lock your doors, keep valuables out of sight and preferably leave promptly.

When you park your car, always consider your location, especially if you are returning to the car in the dark. Avoid dark streets or quiet neighbourhoods or parking next to vans. Have your keys out before you get to the car; your exit will be quicker and you have a weapon in your hand.

2. BREAKDOWNS

If you break down on an expressway, use the emergency phone but sit away from the vehicle until help arrives. Leave the vehicle unlocked so that if you had to you could run to the car and lock yourself in. If you break down in a suburban street, lock the doors and call for help on your mobile. Don't take a lift with another car; ask that driver to send help to you.

It's really important to keep your car in good repair to avoid putting yourself in unnecessary danger. If you are undertaking a journey through remote areas you should be prepared for the worst-case scenario: a breakdown at night with no passing traffic or network coverage. Pack warm clothes or blankets, walking shoes, food, water and a torch. Tell someone your proposed route and check your petrol, all the fluids under the bonnet and tyre pressure. If you break down it is preferable not to sleep in the car but to 'camp' somewhere nearby.

3. STRANGERS

If someone flags you down for help while you are driving, stay in the car and help by calling 000 on your mobile. Unfortunately a lot of predators feign illness or infirmity to get your attention, or even ask for assistance in getting into their car.

Never pick up a hitchhiker or be one.

THE PERFECT REVERSE PARK

1.

Indicate that you intend to park. Position your car next to, and slightly forward of, the car you are want to park behind. Check for pedestrians.

2.

Slowly reverse and turn the wheel towards the curb. Watch the line of the curb out of your rear window. Once the curb has 'disappeared' from your driver's side corner of the rear window, slowly start to straighten the car by turning the wheel in the opposite direction.

3.

If you have watched the curb line in your rear window you shouldn't even need to tinker with the position of the car. Check that the cars at either end of your perfect park have room to take off.

ROAD RAGE

Road rage has an amazing array of manifestations: tailgating, rude gestures, swearing, overtaking on the left, swerving between lanes, speeding and overuse of the horn.

1. AVOID CONTACT

Don't make eye contact with the aggressor; try to drive safely out of the aggressor's way and avoid returning rude gestures. If the temptation to respond is overwhelming, give a friendly wave. The aggressor will spend the next ten kilometres trying to work out where you have met.

2. FIND A CROWD

If you are being followed, drive to a police station, hospital entrance or service station. If you are in a remote area keep driving and, if it is possible to do so safely, call 000 on your mobile. Get your passenger to write down or memorise the aggressor's number plate. If there is no crowd to be found, put your hazard lights on and keep your hand on the horn.

3. AVOID BECOMING AN AGGRESSOR YOURSELF

Try to leave home five minutes earlier than you need for your journey. Drive within the speed limit and let cars in if traffic is merging.

COMPUTER BUZZ WORDS

1. Bit – the smallest unit of information on a computer. Eight of them make a byte.
2. Blog – a website showcasing someone's life or thoughts.
3. Bug – originally an insect fried in a computer's electrical circuit, this now describes an error missed in program testing.

SELF-DEFENCE

Enrol in a self-defence course to boost your fitness and self-confidence, and buy a personal alarm or whistle. If your attacker is clearly just after your bag, let him have it. If, however, he has a more serious intent, you should also 'let him have it' with the full force of self-defence. It is more likely that you will be physically assaulted by someone you know than a stranger. These Three of the Best can be applied to anyone.

1. RUN

It is vital to react immediately to any attack so that you are not dragged to another site or into a car. If you can get away you should run and start shouting 'HELP'. If 'help' is not getting you any attention, try shouting 'FIRE'. If you are being pursued and running out of breath, put a large object that you can see over, like a parked car, between you and the attacker and 'play' get-me-if-you-can. Keep shouting for help and at the attacker.

2. COUNTER-ATTACK

If you are grabbed from the front, poke your attacker in the eyes with your fingers, hit under the nose with your hand, punch a clenched fist to the adam's apple and kick in the groin with your foot or knee. If you are attacked from behind, try a strong elbow to the ribs, the heel of your shoe to the toes or bend back the attacker's fingers.

You need to do whatever you do as hard as you possibly can. It is most likely that your legs are stronger than your upper body. If you don't exert enough force you may not break free and only inflame the attacker's anger. You may only get one chance with the element of surprise, so make it a good one. Use your umbrella, handbag or car keys as a weapon.

3. BUNKER

If you get away but can't find safety, get under a parked car. It is better to be on your back so you can hold onto something if you have to and kick out with your legs to counter further attack. At the very least you are hopefully making yourself too difficult to be worth the trouble. Keep shouting and try to make a 000 call.

NOT-TO-MISS MEDICAL CHECK-UPS

1. CERVIX AND BREAST

The pap test checks for changes to cells of the cervix that might lead to cancer. You should have a test done by a doctor every two years if you have ever been sexually active and you are aged between 18 and 70 years. You should still have the test even if you have been vaccinated. You can also have the test done at a community or women's health or family planning clinic. Most women who develop cervical cancer have never had a test or have not had one for a long time, so put it in your diary. Call the National Cervical Screening Information Line on 13 15 56.

While you're at the GP, have a breast examination. The rate of breast cancer is very high; slightly more than one in ten women will have breast cancer before the age of 75. Nine out of ten women who have breast cancer don't have a family history of it. Ask the doctor to show you how to do a self-examination so you can do check-ups between professional visits.

If you are aged between 50 and 69 you can take part in the BreastScreen Australia program in your state or territory. Call 13 20 50 to book a free screening.

Encourage a female friend to have a check-up in the same week and then meet for an 'all bits done' lunch or dinner. Find out more about both tests at www.cancerscreening.gov.au.

2. CHOLESTEROL

You should know what your cholesterol level is because if it's not in the normal range (3.5 to 5.5) then you are a candidate for coronary disease. You will need to give a fasting blood sample, so it might be easier to book an appointment first thing in the morning. You can't eat for 12 hours before and that includes oral contraceptives or vitamin supplements.

3. SKIN

Your doctor, dermatologist or local skin clinic can give you a full body skin cancer check-up. Go once a year or more often if you have noticed changes to moles or freckles, or any UFOs (unidentified funny objects). Don't forget to check the soles of your feet, ears, back, under bra straps and in your hair part. Australia still has the highest rate of skin cancer in the world, so you can't be too careful.

APOSTROPHE SURVIVAL

1.

For single nouns, put the apostrophe before the s to show possession – The guinea pig's bowl is empty.

For single nouns ending in 's', put the apostrophe before *or* after the s to show possession – Octavius' room was a nightmare *or* Octavius's room was a nightmare.

2.

For plural nouns, put the apostrophe before the s to show possession — The children's lunchboxes were a delight to see.

For plural nouns ending in s, you put the apostrophe after the S to show possession — The ladies' luncheon was a strange affair.

3.

The apostrophe also moonlights in contracted words, or words made up of two smaller words — it's = it is; you're = you are; and we're = we are.

GLOBAL MEANINGS

1. Globalisation. The movement of people and goods due to greater economic integration and trade in a seemingly borderless world where some countries have prospered and others have suffered.

2. Global warming. A 'blanket' of water vapour, carbon dioxide and other naturally and industrially occurring 'greenhouse' gases that traps the sun's radiation in the earth's atmosphere, creating a warmer planet.

3. Globule. A small, spherical body, usually seen hanging from a young child's nose.

MOBILE PHONES

Mobile phones are a mixed blessing. They can be an unnecessary financial drain, but on the other hand they can give a feeling of security.

1.

Enter your emergency contact, listed clearly as such, in your mobile. In case of accident it's the first place doctors, nurses and so on will look for contact information.

2.

When travelling, take mobile phone pictures of the people you're with, particularly children, every morning. If anything should happen to them, you'll have valuable information, including what they were wearing.

3.

Take your phone with you when driving, but don't chat on it as you drive along. It's there in case of breakdown or accident.

DOWNTIME

ENTERTAINING IDEAS

It's fun to invite people over, but only if we make it as stress-free as possible. A perceived inability to cook should never be an excuse not to entertain, because reaching out to friends, inviting them into your home, ensures that we keep friendships alive.

If you hate to cook, order home-delivered pizzas. That way you only have to make a salad: buy mixed salad leaves and make a dressing of two-thirds virgin olive oil to one-third red or white wine vinegar, shaken in a small jar with salt and pepper. Buy a cake or ice-cream for dessert. Barbecued chickens and some bought potato salad with good bread, a green salad, and maybe some cheese is another easy option.

But cooking food for a party is easy as long as you follow the golden rule: do as little as possible at the last minute. The trick is to prepare as much as you can in advance either the day before or, even better, a few weeks ahead, so that you have food stashed in the freezer that only has to be defrosted or heated.

Here are Three of the Best recipes entertaining either a small or large group with minimum effort on the day.

$\mathcal{1}.$ STARTER

ANCHOVY FRITTERS

These are great for parties and are substantial enough to take the place of a sit-down first course at lunch and dinner parties. Complicated entrees are one of the banes of entertaining with all the serving, clearing and washing-up involved. Much easier to put down a plate of these with some salsa or chilli sauce for dipping and some paper napkins and let guests help themselves.

3⅓ cups plain flour
500g mashed potato
50g butter, diced
35g caster sugar
14g dried yeast
4 eggs
2 x 80g jars of anchovy fillets (you need about 40)
vegetable oil for deep frying

Put flour in a large bowl and make a well in the centre. Add the potato, butter, sugar and yeast and mix together with a wooden spoon. Add eggs, one at a time, stirring in before adding the next. When thoroughly combined, cover the bowl with plastic wrap and set aside for ten minutes. Drain anchovies and then cut roughly into halves, setting aside. Pour enough oil in a deep-fryer or deep saucepan to come about halfway up the sides. Heat oil until hot enough to sizzle when a teaspoon of the mix is added. To fry the fritters, take a small amount of the mixture (about one dessertspoon) in your hands and press half an anchovy into the centre then drop it carefully into the oil. Don't worry about the shape –

you should have fritters about 2.5 centimetres in diameter. Fry in batches of about four at a time and drain on a tray covered with kitchen paper. Makes 60 to 80.

These freeze well and are great for reheating and serving with impromptu drinks. To reheat, tip onto a baking tray lined with baking paper and put into a preheated 180°C oven for about ten minutes. Serve with a bought tomato salsa, or sweet chilli sauce.

2. MAIN

MASSAMAN CURRY

This is another great party dish because it is served in bowls and eaten with a fork, so there is no need to sit at a table.

1 tablespoon vegetable oil
1 large brown onion, chopped
4 tablespoons massaman curry paste
800ml coconut cream
2 tablespoons fish sauce
half a fresh pineapple, peeled and chopped into cubes about 2.5cm
50g unsalted peanuts, lightly toasted
½ tablespoon salt
3 tablespoons caster sugar
1kg chuck steak cut into largish pieces, about 4cm square and 2cm thick
100g pumpkin, cut into chunks
100g potato, thickly sliced
rice and coriander for serving

In a deep pan, heat oil and cook onion until softened, then add curry paste and stir for several minutes over medium heat. Add 125 millimetres (half a cup) of coconut cream and stir. Bring to a simmer and add fish sauce. Bring back to a simmer and add pineapple, peanuts, salt and sugar. Pour in the remaining coconut cream, bring to simmering point, then carefully add the meat. Simmer, uncovered, on a very low heat for about one-and-a-half hours, then add the pumpkin and potato. Continue to cook until meat is very tender – it will take about another hour. Serve with rice and chopped coriander leaves. Serves six.

If making for a crowd, double the quantity for 12, or triple for 18. If freezing, put into several containers so that you do not end up with a huge frozen mass that will take ages to defrost.

3. DESSERT

PISTACHIO MERINGUES

These make a lovely sweet to hand around with a bowl of thick cream at parties – or you can make it without the pistachios and convert the meringues to Eton Mess, a delicious dessert for more formal occasions. Meringues will keep well for a couple of weeks in an airtight container.

4 egg whites
1 cup sugar
50g pistachio kernels

Preheat oven to 130°C. Line two baking trays with baking paper. Using an electric mixer, beat egg whites until stiff. Continue beating while gradually adding the sugar. When the mixture is stiff and glossy, fold in the pistachio nuts. Use a tablespoon to put dollops of meringue on the baking trays, transfer to the oven and cook for about one-and-a half to two hours – break a meringue in half to check that the inside is dry. Turn off the heat and leave in the oven to cool. Makes about 25.

For Eton Mess, break each meringue into three or four pieces. Whip 300 millilitres cream with about two teaspoons of icing sugar. Put the meringues in a serving bowl with some fresh berries, or some sliced banana and passionfruit pulp (or any other fruit combination you fancy), then fold through the whipped cream. If you like you can use half Greek yoghurt mixed with the cream, or even all Greek yoghurt instead of cream. Serves eight.

GETTING OUT OF YOUR COMFORT ZONE

1.

If you normally read novels or biographies, try some poetry. Les Murray is a leading Australian poet and a good one to start with. Luke Davies is a brilliant younger Australian poet – his collection of love poems, *Totem*, was the *Age* Book of the Year in 2004. Or try oft-quoted poems such as British poet, W.H. Auden's Pulitzer prizewinner 'The Age of Anxiety', or US-born British poet T.S. Eliot's 'The Waste Land'. Second-hand bookshops are a good source of poetry books.

2.

Many of us rate public speaking as one of our greatest fears. Do a Toastmasters International course – there are branches all over Australia and probably one in easy reach of your home (check your phonebook). You don't need to join a club, just do one of the Toastmasters Speechcraft courses. But the clubs have other activities as well and can be a good way to meet people of both sexes while building your confidence.

3.

Try a new experience. It might be climbing the Sydney Harbour Bridge, parachuting out of a plane, going to live in another country for a year, volunteering (check out who needs help in your area), or learning a new skill. There are all sorts of minor changes you can make if you feel you're in a rut: buy a different newspaper, switch radio stations, or if you normally listen to Mozart try some rock or vice versa. As they say, a change is as good as a holiday!

IDEAS FOR CREATING YOUR OWN NETWORK

1. BOOK GROUP

Ring up a friend who you know loves books as much as you do, then each of you ring three more friends to kick-start your book group. There is more chance of ongoing success if everyone lives within the same locality. Plan to first meet at your place on a night or weekend one month in advance. Tell everyone your book choice and author. Try to pick something, at least to start with, that is readily available in libraries for those people who can't buy books. Put together a simple supper or afternoon tea. Be prepared to speak up first and explain why you picked the book and what you thought of it, so as to get the conversation going. Maybe a short list of questions will kick the debate along, so try the author's or publisher's website for inspiration. Always arrange the next meeting before everyone heads home. Put together a contact list with everyone's name, address, email and phone number as well as a running list of the book choices.

If you can't think of a bookaholic friend to ring, talk to your local bookshop. They might run a book group or know of one in your area.

Variations on a theme: poetry club, the novels of a particular author, or the nominees for the Miles Franklin award.

2. FILM GROUP

Ring up a friend who is a movie buff like you and try to think of a group of about five people for a monthly movie get-together. If you need to start smaller, that will work too. Arrange a set time, such as the first Tuesday of every month, for your viewing. Investigate cheaper days at your local cinema and loyalty programs. Some cinemas also have baby-friendly sessions if your group is all new mums. Find a cafe that you can use for your 'Margaret and David' suppers afterwards.

Variations on a theme: pre-arranged DVDs at home are a cheaper and child-friendly option.

3. WALKING GROUP

Ring around some friends of similar fitness and ask them to meet you at a designated spot. Make it overwhelmingly convenient, such as straight after the school drop-off or a lunchtime date central to everyone's work. Decide on some walking routes. Factor in a warm-up (gentle walking and stretching stations), a work-out (aim to power walk for 30 minutes-plus, depending on fitness and time constraints) and a cool-down (gentle walking and more stretching). Include some hills or stairs. Remind everyone to bring a drink bottle and good walking shoes.

Variations on a theme: walking with prams, running, walking and running, bike-riding or bushwalking.

BRA FITTINGS

1.

Over 80 percent of women wear the wrong size bra. Set aside time to have yourself measured and fitted by an expert at a department or speciality store once every couple of years, or after weight fluctuation.

2.

If you can't get to an expert, measure your girth under your breasts to determine your body size. If it's 70 centimetres then you're a 10, 75 centimetres then you're a 12, 80 centimetres then you're a 14, or 85 centimetres then you're a 16.

3.

Measure your girth over your breasts to determine your bust size. Take your body size measurement away from your bust size measurement. If that result is 13 centimetres or less then you're an A, 15 centimetres then you're an B, 17 centimetres then you're a C, 20 centimetres or more and you're a D.

INTERNET SHOPPING

Shopping online is a growing phenomenon.
We've still got a long way to go before we catch up
with the UK and the US, but hundreds of thousands
of Australians have been quick to see the
advantages: no driving, no parking problems, no
queuing and no foot-slogging to find exactly what you
want. It's the new version of 'let your fingers
do the walking'.

The big one, of course, is eBay, and nowadays it's not just second-hand goods — there's lots of new stuff too. Amazon.com, the giant US book retailer, got shoppers used to the idea, then we started buying our travel and accommodation online because it's so easy to suss out exactly what we want. And it's gone on from there with many of us now doing food shopping online. You can even order a Tasmanian lobster home-delivered or send one gift-wrapped (make sure the recipient will be at home!).

Deals Direct is our largest online department store, but there are numerous others. Gillett's is an online jeweller where you can browse to your heart's content without being subject to the hard sell common in some jewellery chain stores. It's also possible to access overseas fashion not available here: if there's a label that you like, do a search and see what comes up. You can find good deals on cosmetics too and it's easy to compare prices — www.adorebeauty.com.au is a good beauty website. If you can't get to Paris, visit www.olivolga.com for truly enchanting fragrances and wonderfully fanciful jewellery that seems out of this world. And shopping online is a boon if you live in the country and can't get the herbs and spices you want for a special dish; try Herbie's Spices (www.herbies.com.au) or Screaming Seeds (www.screamingseeds.com.au).

With any online purchase, though, it's important to check shipping costs to make sure that any price saving isn't more than eaten up by the cost of getting it to your home address.

Here are Three of the Best precautions you should take to safeguard your interests.

Check the seller's refund and returns policy plus the warranty on goods where applicable. Successful mail-order firms like EziBuy and Damart built their business by a no-problem refund policy, and it's essential to be assured of this when dealing with an online retailer. It's a case of buyer beware, though, when dealing with a private individual.

2.

When giving credit card details, make sure the page is secure. Check that the address at the top of the page begins 'https' (instead of 'http'), or look for a closed padlock on the bottom left-hand corner of the screen. If you plan on doing a lot of online shopping, it's worth having a separate credit card with a low limit for the purpose. If you want to make a major purchase you can top up the card with a cash transfer beforehand.

3.

Print a copy of your order before you send it.

SITES FOR INSPIRATION

Need a new direction in health, study or work?

1. www.health.gov.au

2. www.courses.com.au

3. www.smallbusiness.gov.au

STAYING PASSIONATE

No relationship stays the same over the years, and
sexual desire is likely to wax and wane in a long-term
partnership. Psychotherapist Esther Perel (author of
*Mating In Captivity: Reconciling the Erotic and the
Domestic*) believes that many of the factors we think of
as contributing to a good relationship – such as
friendship, stability, intimacy and security – go against
sexual desire, which thrives on mystery and
unpredictability. People can be too close, too merged
in each other's lives for there to be any of the
separateness that spurs desire.

So, it's not too little emotional intimacy that kills
passion, but sometimes too much. If we have a strong
emotional connection with our partner we're not going
to want to let that go, so it's important to keep lust alive
by recognising the need to plan for sex.

If you have children, don't make them responsible
for a dwindling sex life. Children thrive best in families
where parents' relationship with each other is stronger
than the parent–child bond. One day children will want
to lead their own lives and it's important that they have
the space to develop in their own right. Here are Three
of the Best ways to stay passionate:

1.

Remember that it's quality not quantity that counts with sex.

2.

Go out to dinner (without the kids) and escape the domestic environment where other concerns can intrude. Try to go away sometimes — just the two of you — and get away from your everyday lives. If you can't go out stay in and cook one of the best seduction meals — see the next Three of the Best.

3.

Plan for sex. If you wait for it to be spontaneous, it might not happen.

COURSES FOR A SEDUCTION MENU

This menu works well for a romantic dinner because you can make the dessert in advance, even the day before. You can also prepare the potato dish ahead of time and slip it into the oven 45 minutes before you want to serve the main course. The dressing for the oysters can be made in advance and kept in the fridge.

1. OYSTERS WITH LIME AND SOY DRESSING

Mix 2 teaspons of soy sauce, the juice of half a lime, a teaspoon of finely chopped fresh ginger, and one deseeded finely chopped chilli. Spoon a little over each of two dozen oysters and serve immediately.

2. FILLET STEAK WITH MEDLEY OF MUSHROOMS AND POTATO GRATIN

First prepare the potato gratin: Heat oven to 180°C. Grease a small casserole dish or springform tin. Peel and finely slice four medium potatoes and finely chop one garlic clove. Arrange layers of potato slices in the dish mixed with the garlic, a light sprinkling of nutmeg, salt and pepper to taste, and some diced butter (about 60g). Bring three-quarters of a cup of milk to the boil and pour over the potatoes. Put in the oven and cook for about 45 minutes.

Next the mushroom medley: About 15 minutes before you aim to serve dinner, slice a variety of mushrooms — whatever looks good in your local fruit and veg shop. Heat one tablespoon of oil and about the same amount of butter in a non-stick pan. Add the mushrooms and sauté over medium heat for about five minutes.

And then the fillet steak: You will need two pieces of fillet steak about 5 centimetres thick. Press some freshly ground black pepper into the steaks. Heat a frying pan (or a chargrill pan brushed with a little oil works well) over medium heat. Add a thin film of olive oil, then the steaks and cook three minutes a side for medium-rare. Rest the steaks for about five minutes. If you like, make a sauce from the pan juices: add a nut of butter and a few drops of Worcestershire sauce to the pan. Use a wooden spoon to stir in the pan juices and add a little cream (about one tablespoon). Serve under or over the steaks.

3. FOR DESSERT, MAKE SCRUMPTIOUS CHOCOLATE CAKE

See 'Chocolate treats to make at home' on page 206 in FUEL.

WAYS TO MAKE NEW FRIENDS

1. WORK

Working in a big organisation with lots of employees of both sexes is the best way to widen your circle. You may even meet the love of your life if you haven't already. Small offices or, worse, jobs where you work on your own, say as a nanny, home nurse or GP, are okay if you have a large circle of friends, but working in this sort of environment eliminates the most fertile territory for meeting new people. So, for instance, if you're a doctor or nurse, go for a job in a big general hospital. Many organisations have social clubs or organise groups to play touch footy or go for power walks in the lunch hour. And even if there is nothing this organised there are likely to be employee social events during the year, a staff canteen, or drinks after work at a local watering hole. Plus there's nothing to stop you organising something yourself and spreading the word.

2. ENTERTAIN

This is essential to maintaining friendships, but it's also a way you can bring people you don't know well, but would like to know better, closer. If you're having a party, try to include someone outside your usual circle. That way your close friends are meeting someone new as well. And anyone you invite is likely to reciprocate — otherwise, forget about them!

3. GET INVOLVED

If you want to meet someone special, don't make that your sole focus, although if it is you could try some of the internet dating sites. Widening your circle of friends in general terms and having an active social life increases your chances, but it may not be enough if you get to a point in life where almost everyone you know is in a relationship.

In our twenties, many of our friends are single and people we meet at clubs and parties are likely to be single too. But if you want to end up in a permanent relationship, it's important not to get stuck in a relationship that's going nowhere and waste these years. Read *He's Just Not That Into You* by Greg Behrendt and Liz Tuccillo and stop making excuses for men who aren't really interested.

Once you get to the stage when — through divorce, death or wasting time in losing relationships — you're the lone single woman in your group, it's not much use enrolling in dance classes; there aren't likely to be any stray men on the dance floor (although it's how Mma Grace Makutsi meets her fiancé Phuti Radiphuti in Alexander McCall Smith's *In the Company of Cheerful Ladies*). Sailing and rowing clubs and sporting activities involving men are more likely, and it's worth checking out local evening courses. Men enrol in anything from cooking to navigating. And clubs such as Toastmasters (see 'Getting out of your comfort zone' on page 316) attract people of both sexes. At the very least, there's the bonus of a new skill.

FILM DIRECTORS TO NAME DROP (FEMALE)

1. Gillian Armstrong: *My Brilliant Career*, *Oscar and Lucinda*, *Charlotte Gray*.
2. Jane Campion: *Sweetie*, *The Piano*, *In the Cut*.
3. Sofia Coppola: *The Virgin Suicides*, *Lost in Translation*, *Marie Antoinette*.

FILM DIRECTORS TO NAME DROP (MALES)

1. David Lynch: *The Elephant Man*, *Blue Velvet*, *Mulholland Drive*.
2. Martin Scorsese: *Taxi Driver*, *Raging Bull*, *Shine a Light*.
3. Steven Soderbergh: sex, lies and videotape, *Erin Brockovich*, *Solaris*.

MOOD MUSIC

Researchers from McGill University in Montreal used brain scans to research why different sorts of music suit different activities. Personal preferences obviously come into it, but the study identified broad styles for various activities. For instance, household chores aren't quite as boring while listening to music with an energetic beat, while low-tempo instrumental music is suitable for studying because it doesn't distract. Here are some of the selections reported in the *Sydney Morning Herald* (25–26 August 2007):

1. HOUSEHOLD CHORES

Sarah McLachlan, *Wintersong*; Buena Vista Social Club; Tommy Flanagan, *Trio & Sextet*; Vivaldi, *Four Seasons*; AC/DC, *Back In Black*; McFly, 'Baby's Coming Back'.

2. EXERCISE

Avril Lavigne; Village People; Arrested Development; Creedence Clearwater Revival; The Temptations; Talking Heads; Madonna, 'Hung Up'; Irene Cara, 'What a Feeling'.

3. ROMANCING

Amerie; Akon, *Konvicted*; The Postal Service; Ella Fitzgerald, *Sings the Cole Porter Songbook*; Barry White, *All-time Greatest Hits*; Debussy, *Piano Works*.

PICNIC MEALS

Food tastes better when we eat outdoors: the fresh air, the scent of grass and trees and the feeling of relaxation all add to the flavour. A picnic spread can be simple – bread, cheese and some ripe peaches – or more complicated, but it should be easy to transport (with a few ice bricks in hot weather) and serve.

1. ZUCCHINI LOAF

1 cup self-raising flour, sifted
125g parmesan cheese, grated
½ cup vegetable oil
4 eggs, lightly beaten
3 zucchini, trimmed and coarsely grated
1 onion, finely chopped
2 cloves garlic, finely chopped

Grease a loaf tin and dust lightly with flour. Preheat oven to 180°C. Combine the flour and parmesan, then add the oil and eggs. Stir until combined. Mix in the zucchini, onion and garlic. Scrape the mixture into the tin and bake for about 50 minutes until golden brown. Cool in the tin for ten minutes, then turn out onto a cake rack to finish cooling. Serves eight.

2. ABERDEEN SAUSAGE

Bring along some potato salad and crusty bread to serve with this.

500g minced beefsteak (top quality with little fat)
250g bacon, finely chopped
1 egg, beaten
1 tablespoon tomato paste
salt and black pepper to taste
2 cups fresh breadcrumbs, plus extra for serving

Combine all ingredients. Shape into a roll on a lightly floured surface. Wrap the roll securely in foil, then wrap again in another sheet of foil. Put into a pot of boiling water, then cover and leave to simmer for two hours. To serve, cool then roll in the extra breadcrumbs and cut into thin slices. Serves six.

_3._ PINEAPPLE AND CARROT LOAF

No picnic is complete without a sweet treat to finish. This recipe makes two loaves, so put one in the freezer.

2 cups plain flour
2 teaspoons baking powder
2 level teaspoons bicarbonate of soda
1 teaspoon salt
1 teaspoon ground cinnamon
4 eggs
200ml vegetable oil
2 cups grated carrot
400g crushed tinned pineapple, drained
1½ cups caster sugar
½ cup chopped walnuts

Preheat oven to 170°C (165°C if fan-forced). Grease and line two loaf tins. Sift the flour, baking powder, bicarbonate of soda, salt and cinnamon into a bowl. Add the eggs, oil, carrot, pineapple, sugar and walnuts. Stir to combine. Pour evenly into the tins and bake for 55 minutes, until golden on top and a skewer inserted in the centre comes out clean. Cool in the tins for ten minutes then turn out onto a cake rack to finish cooling.

PRESENTS FOR SOMEONE YOU DON'T KNOW WELL

1. BOOK OR CD VOUCHER

If you choose a particular book rather than giving a gift voucher, make sure to include an exchange docket because it's very hard to choose the right book for someone, even if you know them well. The same goes for music. Major record chains such as HMV will post out vouchers if you prefer to order by phone. That way you won't even have to leave the house except to buy a card, but maybe not even for that. It's a good idea to buy a few cards next time you're browsing in the card section, that way you'll always have one on hand.

2. CONSUMABLES

If you don't know someone well, you won't know what they're likely to be lacking in the household goods department. And let's face it: by the time we reach a certain age, we already have cupboards full of the stuff. So choose something that we're always going to run out of. For example, scented soaps (L'Occitane and Crabtree & Evelyn are two of the best ranges), a bottle of wine, or a bottle of spirits, perhaps something a little out of the basic range, for instance, Bison Grass Vodka or another of the flavoured vodkas, or Bombay Sapphire Gin.

3. EDIBLES

If you enjoy cooking, make some biscuits, either sweet to serve with coffee or tea, or savoury to serve with drinks. Pack them in an airtight container then put the container plus a copy of the recipe into a decorative box.

Here are three of our favourite recipes for giving (see also, in FUEL section, chocolate truffles in 'Chocolate treats to make at home' on page 208, and caramelised walnuts in 'Things to add to salads' on page 211).

LEMON CLOVE COOKIES

This is based on an Alice Waters recipe from the *Chez Panisse Menu Cookbook*.

250g butter
¾ cup sugar
1 teaspoon vanilla essence
1 egg
zest of 1 lemon
2⅓ cups plain flour, sifted
1 level teaspoon ground cloves
some whole cloves for storing

In a food processor, cream the butter and sugar until light and fluffy. Add vanilla, egg and lemon zest and process briefly until combined. Add the sifted flour and ground cloves and process so that you have a soft dough. Spread some plastic wrap on a board then take about half the mixture and roll into a cylinder about 2.5 to 3 centimetres in diameter. Wrap the cylinder in the plastic and chill in the fridge for at least two hours, overnight if you like. Do the same with the other half of the mixture. When ready to bake, preheat oven to 180°C. Line two baking trays with baking paper. Unwrap the cylinders and, using a sharp, heavy knife, cut into slices about 1-centimetre thick. Put the cookies onto the baking trays with at least 1 centimetre between them. Bake for 10 to 15 minutes until they are light golden brown on top and slightly darker underneath. Cool on the baking trays or on cake racks. Pack into an airtight container with a few whole cloves scattered around. Makes about 50.

JOAN'S CHEESE AND CORIANDER BISCUITS

1 cup plain flour, sifted
2 tablespoons self-raising flour, sifted
1 small red chilli, deseeded and finely chopped
2 tablespoons coriander, finely chopped
125g butter
125g vintage cheddar, grated
2 tablespoons grated parmesan

Put the flours, chilli, coriander and butter into a food processor and process until combined. Scrape down the sides if necessary and add the cheeses. Process to combine. Spread some plastic wrap on a board and roll the mixture into two cylinders 2.5 to 3 centimetres in diameter. Wrap each in plastic wrap and chill in the fridge for at least three hours. When ready to bake, preheat the oven to 170°C. Line two baking trays with baking paper. Using a heavy knife, cut the cylinder into slices about 1-centimetre thick and put on the baking trays at least 1-centimetre apart. Cook for 20 to 25 minutes until light golden brown. Makes about 60.

TRICIA'S CHEESE BISCUITS

These tasty morsels are incredibly easy to make.

Using equal quantities of sifted plain flour, grated parmesan and butter, plus a good pinch of cayenne pepper, process all ingredients until a ball forms. Using the same method as the previous recipe, roll into cylinders and refrigerate for at least two hours. Preheat oven to 180°C. Line two baking trays with baking paper. Cut the cylinder into slices about 1-centimetre thick and put on the trays about 1-centimetre apart. Cook for 15 minutes or until light golden brown. Using 120 grams each of flour, parmesan and butter, this makes about 50.

UNDIES

1. SEX SHOPS

Go with a friend and have fun checking out the range — best if you're looking for something really saucy.

2. TARGET

Great value basics for all shapes and sizes.

3. LA PERLA

Madonna started the trend for lingerie as clothing, and this range is so gorgeous it's a shame to keep it under wraps. Ada Masotti, a concierge, started making corsets for wealthy women in the 1950s and her brand is now an Italian fashion icon. Princess Di was among the celebrities who delight in its sheer luxury. Featuring handmade lace and embroidery, La Perla is not for the faint-hearted or the cash-strapped, with many items costing upwards of $300. If you want to splurge you can also check out exorbitantly priced but exquisite French lingerie labels such as Cadolle, Fifi Chachnil, Chantal Thomass, Princesse Tam Tam, and Marlies Dekkers on the net, but even knowing the European equivalent of your size (see page 339) is no guarantee of correct fit as sizes vary between labels.

STANDARD SIZING CONVERTERS

1. Clothes

AUST	US	UK	EUROPEAN
8	4	6	34
10	6	8	36
12	8	10	38
14	10	12	40
16	12	14	42

2. Shoes

AUST	US	EUROPEAN
6	6	37
7	7	38
8	8	39.5
9	9	40.5
10	10	42

3. Small – 10–12

   Medium – 12–14

   Large – 14–16

STAND UP

DISCLAIMER

Every effort has been made to ensure that the contents of this section are as accurate as possible. Neither the authors nor the publishers can accept any responsibility for any loss suffered as a result of this material. Always consult a legal professional.

HOT DOCUMENTS

1. WILLS

Your will is one of the most important documents you ever make, so it is a good idea to get it right. You can make a will yourself and there are kits available at newsagents and post offices for that purpose. You don't need to use a lawyer to make a will, but if there is anything complicated about what you propose then it is probably a good idea.

If you don't write a will then your assets will be distributed according to a set formula (surviving spouse and children, parents, brothers and sisters, close blood relatives and, if all else fails, the government). To avoid all of that, your will names the people (the beneficiaries) who will get your property and personal possessions after your death. You can make provision for your land, car, shares, insurance policies, bank accounts, jewellery or anything else you own.

Your superannuation can be dealt with separately to your other assets. Super can be paid out in accordance with your binding death benefit nomination or, if you haven't completed a nomination with your fund or your fund doesn't offer that option, it will be distributed to your dependants which will include your children and spouse or ex-spouse if you are separated but haven't divorced yet.

If you leave your spouse or children out of your will it's possible they could make a *Family Provision Act* claim.

Your will must be in writing (handwritten or typed). Your will should be signed and dated by you and your signature must be witnessed by two people who are not the beneficiaries or the spouses of the beneficiaries. If some part of this process is not done properly, a court has the discretion to declare the will invalid.

At some stage you might need to change your will. If you have changed your mind then you might need to write a new will or, if the change is minor, you can create an extra document called a codicil (it also must be signed and witnessed). If you made your will before you were married then it is ineffective after you tie the knot (unless the will sets out that it was made in contemplation of marriage). You should make a new will if you have become divorced or separated.

Store your will in a safe place such as with your solicitor or executor/s (the person named in the will who you have checked is happy to look after your affairs). Make sure you keep a copy yourself with a note on it as to the whereabouts of the original.

2. POWER OF ATTORNEY

This document appoints another person of your choosing to act for you on financial matters. The attorney can be appointed for a specific purpose or generally. The attorney can act for you indefinitely (unless you cancel it while you possess mental capacity) or for a nominated period of time, for example, while you are in hospital or overseas. If you lose the ability to make decisions or die then this general power of attorney no longer operates.

If you want an attorney to continue to act for you after you have lost mental capacity then you need to sign a document called an enduring power of attorney. This document must be witnessed, but not by the attorney, and a certificate of your understanding of the document must also be completed by the witness. This document needs to be made before you lose the capacity to manage your own affairs.

In other words, both the general and enduring powers of attorney need you to plan ahead for someone you trust to make decisions on your behalf. That person must be trustworthy, over the age of 18 and have the capacity and time to take on the task. If you don't have someone in that category, the public trustee or a private trustee company can do the job for a fee.

3. LETTER OF DEMAND

You may need to write one of these or you might receive one on a solicitor's stationary. Essentially, these letters state that someone (the debtor) owes someone else (the creditor) some money. Usually the letter ends with 'unless the sum of $X is received within 14 days from the date of this letter legal proceedings will be commenced without further notice'.

It is unwise to ignore the letter because if legal proceedings are commenced (you will be served with a statement of claim) and you do owe the money then you could also end up paying interest and legal costs. If you don't owe the money you should set this out in a letter to the creditor with the reasons that the money is not owed.

If you owe the money but can't afford to pay it off in one go, you can ask the creditor to pay by instalments or come to some other arrangement.

Have a look at www.artslaw.com.au/Legal Information/ DebtRecovery for state-by-state advice.

THE PAPER TRAIL

1. IMPORTANT DOCUMENTS

Documents should generally be kept for at least seven years. It's a good idea to buy folders or suspension files and keep your documents by way of subject matter, such as taxation, superannuation and bank statements. The exceptions to the seven-year rule of thumb are documents that have a limited life span, such as some insurance policies, or documents that need to be kept for life, such as a certificate of marriage or certificate of divorce.

In a fire-resistant box, keep photocopies of your passport's front page, driver's license and important 'plastic' such as credit and Medicare cards.

2. FILE NOTES

Every time you have an important conversation you should make a file note. A file note is a written record of what was said and done that you have dated and signed. You might make a file note if you are speaking to someone at your local council about a contentious issue, or talking to a tradesperson about scope of works. You don't have to make notes while you are face to face but you should make the file note as soon as possible afterwards so the note is contemporaneous with the event you are recording. If you are on the phone, make the notes as you go. You could use a week-to-a-page diary and keep all your file notes in one safe spot.

3. CONTRACTS

Never sign a document you don't understand. Never sign a document you have not read several times. Ask lots of questions of the person who has presented the document to you. If you don't understand the answers, ask more questions or get advice from someone else. Don't be afraid to take the document away so you can think about it. If you feel pressured to sign the document on the spot then that is probably a good reason not to do so.

If you sign a contract then you are usually bound by its terms even if you didn't understand it or read it.

MAINTAINING A HEALTHY MARRIAGE

1. Make a date. Once a fortnight, go out as a couple and talk about everything except money, children, housing, relatives or the weather.
2. Make a plan. Brainstorm a written program as to how you could be doing things better on the work–life balancing act.
3. Make a call. If the above seems inadequate, phone today to see a professional counsellor. Call the Family Relationship Advice Line on 1800 050 321.

GENERAL PRINCIPLES OF
FAMILY LAW

1. DIVORCE

This year over 50 000 Australian couples will get a divorce. The process is governed by a piece of legislation called the *Family Law Act*. As it's a federal Act, it applies to all Australian citizens regardless of where you live in the country. In each state there are family law courts and registries; the latter deal with all the administration and paperwork that go on behind the court process. You will be able to get help on procedural matters here.

If you are going through a divorce, you might want to read parts of the Act so you can understand what the court takes into account in making decisions. If you had a taxation problem you probably wouldn't want to read the *Taxation Act*, but the *Family Law Act* is user-friendly. You can find the Act at www.austlii.edu.au.

The general principle is that divorce is 'no fault'. That means the court is not concerned with who is to blame that the marriage has broken down. Some people find this frustrating because they feel their partner is guilty and that the court should acknowledge that failing. In fact the only ground for divorce is the irretrievable breakdown of the relationship demonstrated by twelve months of separation. You may think, like Lord Byron, 'sweet is revenge — especially to women', but in fact success is sweetest. Rise above the blame game and aim to be happier, fitter, more employable and ready for a new relationship.

2. CHILDREN

You and your partner need to decide on the custody arrangements for your children. You can do this by way of an informal arrangement between yourselves or consent orders that you both agree to and file in court (see 'When you both see eye to eye' on page 363). If you and your partner can't agree on a parenting plan then the court will make parenting orders on your behalf.

Arrangements and orders regarding children can be made during the twelve-month separation period before you are divorced. The most important consideration for the family court when making orders is what is in the 'best interests of the child'. The Act is clear that:

- Both parents are responsible for the care and welfare of their children until they reach the age of eighteen.
- Arrangements which involve shared responsibilities and cooperation between the parents are in the best interests of the child.

In most cases, the court presumes that it is in the best interest of a child for parents to have equal shared responsibility, which means you both have an equal role in making decisions about major long-term issues affecting your children. Before you approach the court for parenting orders you will have to go to family dispute resolution (unless there is violence or urgency involved). The Family Relationship Centre provides up to three hours of dispute resolution free of charge (1800 050 321). Have a look at sections 60CA and 60CC of the Act; there is no such thing as a 'usual' arrangement for children under the Act.

Whilst it is normal to feel you want to punish your partner, don't resort to using custody as a weapon. If there is conflict in managing the visits or changeovers between visits, consider some informal supervision of the changeover or the visit itself by a friend or relative. The Australian Children's Contact Service Association provides a supervision network, so have a look at www.accsa.org.au.

As to what forms to use for parenting orders, how to apply and fees, see www.familylawcourts.gov.au or call 1300 352 000. You may need legal advice in applying for parenting orders or if the orders are breached (gone against) by your partner.

3. FINANCES

You and your partner need to decide how to divide up your assets. If you can't jointly resolve your financial dispute then the court will make financial orders based on a number of general principles (have a look at sections 75(2) and 79(4) of the Act):

- what you have (assets, including superannuation) and what you owe (debts)
- direct financial contributions to the marriage (such as wages) and indirect contributions (such as gifts and inheritances)
- non-financial contributions to the marriage (such as caring for children)
- the standard of living during the marriage
- the length of the marriage
- future needs (such as health and age)
- future resources (such as child support and ability to earn)
- the desirability of finalising the financial relationship

You can ask for orders about property division, financial support and, in some circumstances, child support. Before you do, however, you have to follow 'pre-action' procedures, which include attending dispute resolution in an attempt to narrow the issues. You will need legal advice when applying for financial orders or if the orders are breached by your partner.

If you are coming out of a de facto relationship, each state and territory has its own laws and you will need legal advice.

If you cannot agree on child support payments then you may need to apply to the Child Support Agency for help in making arrangements. Even if you have an agreement it's a good idea to lodge it with the agency. Child support is calculated on a formula so go to www.csa.gov.au to look at the child support calculator and determine the payments that apply to your circumstances. Alternatively, you can agree to a higher amount. The agency can collect payments on your behalf. If your spouse is required to and doesn't pay, the Agency can arrange for wage deductions, interception of tax refunds and sale of property proceeds or collection from a bank.

PRENUPTIAL AGREEMENTS

1. WHAT IS IT?

A prenuptial agreement is a legal document between two people as to their financial arrangement if there is a marriage breakdown. The proper term as used in the *Family Law Act* is 'financial agreements'. Some people consider them pessimistic and unromantic. Others consider them essential and a good test of whether two people can handle financial issues in a mature way. Essentially these agreements cover:

- How your property will be dealt with at the end of the marriage.

- Any spousal maintenance at the end of the marriage.
- Any incidental matters (there is no definition in the *Family Law Act* as to what that actually means, but it probably refers to something that is connected with dividing up of property and spousal maintenance).

You will need to get legal advice to enter into such an agreement and for that advice to be independent you should each obtain it from different lawyers. Having an agreement drafted up could cost a few thousand dollars.

2. WHAT YOU NEED

There are two important elements to a prenuptial agreement that make it legally binding or enforceable:

- The agreement has to be signed by both of you.
- The agreement must include a statement saying each of you received independent legal advice about the effect of the agreement on your rights and the fairness of the agreement.

A legal requirement is one thing, but you must, of course, completely understand the agreement and not sign it until you do. Spend some time thinking about what you want in the agreement. You might see the assets that you will bring into the marriage differently from assets you acquire together. You have to imagine that if the agreement is ever needed, the person you are signing it with may no longer be the most important person in your life – in fact, you may loathe them with a passion you never thought possible. Make sure you get the legal advice well in advance of the wedding day (and the lead-up to it) in case it becomes a deal-breaker.

3. OUTCOMES

There are a number of possible endings for a prenuptial agreement, apart from the obvious one of you and your former spouse being bound to follow it.

- The family court can decide the agreement is invalid (or of no effect) if, for example, you didn't get independent legal advice or there was fraud involved in the agreement.
- The court might decide that it is not practicable for the agreement to be followed because of a change in your circumstances.
- You might want to make a second agreement.
- You might want to make a termination agreement ending your prenuptial agreement.
- If one of the parties to the prenuptial agreement dies then the agreement becomes binding on the executor of the estate.

As well as thinking about finances should the marriage end, use this time to think about how you will work out finances while you are married, particularly if you have different money habits. Is it a concern that you have mentally spent your pay packet before you get it while your partner still talks about banking his first pocket money? If you don't know how you both rate in the finance stakes, have a look at the questionnaire at www.getsaving.com.au.

ON SEPARATION

1. RECONCILIATION

Separation is a life-shattering experience. The stages of grief are similar to the experience of death in a family: shock, anger, sadness and acceptance. It's good to talk to family and close friends, but remember that downloading on even your nearest and dearest can be overwhelming for the listener, who may have his or her own marital woes or conflicting loyalties. It's often better to talk to a professional.

Reconciliation counselling is what you go for when your relationship has reached rock bottom and you are thinking about separating, but it's better to consider counselling before you get to that crisis point.

There are a lot of advice and counselling services available. If you are confused about where to turn to first you could start with the Family Relationship Advice Line, a national telephone service to help with relationship or separation issues. Couples, grand-parents, children, step-parents and friends can all access help by calling 1800 050 321 or going to www.familyrelationships.gov.au.

It's okay for your children to see you upset and to talk generally about why you are, but it's not a good idea to go through all the details with them. They are not separation counsellors and they will have their own issues without the burden of yours as well. Whilst you might feel like inflicting GBH on your partner, particularly if the separation is not amicable, he is the father of your children and they are entitled to love and respect him if he has earned it.

2. WHAT TO THINK ABOUT

There are a number of issues that you will need to think about and hopefully discuss with your partner at the time of separation. What you decide to do may only be a temporary measure, but if you can focus on these issues then you and your children will cope better with the changes down the track:

- Where and with whom will our children live?
- How and what will we tell our children?
- How will we share the time with our children?
- How will my partner and I support ourselves and our children?
- Who will pay the bills, rent or mortgage?

- What will happen to the house, car and dog?
- What will I tell family, friends and work colleagues?
- Do I need to reconsider my will and superannuation (in particular the binding death benefit nomination)?
- Do I need any professional help in coming to grips with these questions?

Keep a detailed diary and copies of all your emails as to what you have agreed upon with your partner.

If you and your partner can't afford to live in different locations, you might decide to live in the one house but 'separately and apart'. Naturally, this is not ideal, although it may on a practical level make day-to-day organisation with your children easier. As the only ground for divorce is irretrievable breakdown of the marriage evidenced by twelve months separation, you should probably get some legal advice about living separately under the one roof. It will be necessary to prove the arrangement to the family court.

3. SEPARATION

Once you have thought through some of the preliminary questions you will need to consider what, if any, professional help you now need. Separation counselling is offered by Relationships Australia and you can contact them on 1300 364 277. This kind of help can sort out problems you are having with finances, child support and access, partner conflict and other issues when you are doing it solo.

Legal advice can tell you about your rights if you are in dispute with your partner. You may not need a lawyer if you are both in agreement on issues like custody and property. You can research your legal rights on the internet or in a library. If the issues are complex or acrimonious then you may need legal advice (see 'Ways of hiring and handling a lawyer' on page 367). It's not a good idea to get this sort of advice from friends, even those who have been through a divorce, because everyone's experiences are different and so are the outcomes.

MESSAGES FOR CHILDREN WHEN SEPARATING

1. A child is never to blame for any actions taken by adults.
2. Love for a child is a constant, no matter what else changes.
3. There are lots of different kinds of families and none are any better than others.

GETTING A DIVORCE

Applying for a divorce can be very straightforward: it's in dealing with the issues surrounding children and finances (see 'General principles of family law' on page 349) and maintenance (see 'On spousal maintenance' on page 371) that things get messy. Here are the three basic steps to getting a divorce.

1. THE FORM

Once you have been separated for twelve months, get an 'Application for Divorce' and fill it out. You can do this online at www.familylawcourts.gov.au; there you will find an electronic version of the application and lots of extremely useful and easy-to-read information about all aspects of family law. You will have to swear or affirm the application before a justice of the peace, a person authorised to witness affidavits or a lawyer. You can also pick up an application from a family law registry; for details call 1300 352 000.

Make three copies of the application and any supporting documents that you have attached to it. Also make a copy of your marriage certificate. If that certificate is not in English you will have to get a translation.

2. THE REGISTRY

You must file the original application and two copies of it at a family law registry, along with the copy of the marriage certificate. Keep the third copy of the application in your important documents folder at home. You can file at the registry in person or by post.

When the application is filed you will have to pay a fee. In some circumstances you can request an exemption from the fee by filling out an 'Application for Waiver of Court Fees' form.

You will be given a file number and a hearing date and time.

If you applied for the divorce on your own then the registry will keep the original Application and give you the two copies. It is then necessary for you to serve one sealed copy of the application on your spouse. If your spouse is living in Australia it must be served at least 28 days before the hearing date; if your spouse is living overseas it must be served at least 42 days before the hearing date.

You can serve your spouse by post providing you are confident that he will return the 'Acknowledgement of Service' form to you. Or you can have the application served by hand by a professional process server (involving some cost), a family member or a friend. You can't serve the application in person yourself.

If you applied for the divorce jointly with your spouse then the registry will give you both a sealed copy of the application.

$\mathcal{3}$. THE HEARING

If you don't have a child of the marriage under the age of eighteen years then neither of you need to go to the court hearing. Some people go as part of the process and take a buddy along for support.

If you applied for the divorce jointly with your spouse you don't have to go to the hearing, even if there is a child of the marriage under eighteen years of age.

If you applied for the divorce on your own and there is a child of the marriage under eighteen years of age then you will have to go to the hearing. If you are using a lawyer, the lawyer will go with you to court. If you are going to court on your own, see 'Appearing in court without a lawyer' on page 373.

If all goes well, the court will grant a divorce order. That order becomes final one month and one day after the order is made. Sometimes the court needs more information and you might have to go back again.

Once your divorce becomes final, the court will send you a 'Certificate of Divorce'. That night, plan a dinner out with family and friends to mark this new phase of your life. It's normal to feel bitter, relieved, angry, sad and shell-shocked all at once. Take some time to think about and write down what you want to achieve over the next month (for example, get fit, feel happy) and over the next twelve months (work on creating well-adjusted and happy children, organise a holiday). Don't forget to consider if your will or superannuation needs changing.

WHEN YOU BOTH SEE EYE TO EYE

1. RESOLUTION

If you are in the happy situation of agreeing with your former partner on the important matters of the custody of the children and/or property, both you and your children will be better off emotionally and financially. Even if you agree on most issues and feel comfortable having ongoing contact with your former partner, you might still want to use family dispute resolution services to help you broker the agreements. It's possible for these services to see you and your former partner separately before bringing the arrangement to the table. You can contact the Family Relationship Advice Line on 1800 050 321.

It's a good idea to get your formal arrangements about children and finances in place even if you are on good terms with your partner because that may not always be the case.

If you have concerns about violence or intimidation then a collaborative process is more difficult, and maybe unwise.

2. ABOUT THE CHILDREN

If you and your former partner can agree on the arrangements for your children then there is no need for you to go to court. You have two options. You can create a parenting plan, or consent orders that are approved by the family court.

A **parenting plan** is an agreement you make with your former spouse about how your children will be looked after and supported. It is not a legally enforceable document, but if you want it to be recognised by the court then it needs to be written down, dated and signed by both of you.

Making a parenting plan means agreeing on where your children will live, how day-to-day care will work as well as holidays and special events, financial arrangements for the children, and procedures for changing the plan or implementing longer term issues as the children grow up. You should consider how you and your partner are going to communicate about your children. Some people find it less emotionally charged to use email, text messages or letters rather than the telephone (it also gives you a paper trail of what has been discussed). You might want to think about the boundaries you set for your children and how to keep those consistent from one household to the other, such as: limiting time on the computer and in front of the TV, doing household chores and availability of junk food. If you can agree on the practical day-to-day things then down the track there might be less disagreements, especially if one of the households expands to include a new partner and other children.

The starting point for a parenting plan is the same one that the family court uses: what is in the best interests of the children? It is not a battle plan to inflict pain on your partner. Generally, it is important for children to have a meaningful relationship with both parents by way of a variety of arrangements, such as children spending alternate weeks with each parent or the children living with one parent and spending alternate weekends and one night a week with the other.

The other way to avoid a court appearance in making arrangements for your children is by way of **consent orders**. This is an agreement that is approved by the family court on the provision that the orders you set out are in the best interests of the children. You can use the family court 'Consent Orders Kit' to set out the same sort of arrangements that are put in parenting orders: see www.familylawcourts.gov.au or call 1300 352 000. After you have completed the form in the kit, file it with the family court registry either by post or in person: there is no filing fee involved. Consent orders can be enforced by the court.

3. FINANCES

If you and your former partner can agree about how to resolve your property arrangements then you don't have to go to court. The idea is that you are in control of the process and you don't have the anxiety and cost of a hearing. You have two choices in resolving your property division: a financial agreement or consent orders.

A **financial agreement** can be made at any time before (see 'Prenuptial agreements' on page 353), during or after a marriage. Your financial settlement can include superannuation and financial support. The agreement will be in writing, signed by you and your former partner, and include a certificate setting out that you both had independent advice before you signed it.

A **consent order** is a written agreement between you and your former partner which the court has approved. You can use the family court 'Consent Orders Kit' by going to www.familylawcourts.gov.au or calling 1300 352 000. You then file the order by post or in person; there is no filing fee. The court will make the orders if it is satisfied that what you are seeking is 'just and equitable'.

WAYS OF HIRING AND HANDLING A LAWYER

If you have a friend who has used a lawyer for a similar job, such as resolving a family law dispute, then a word of mouth recommendation might be the way to go. If the friend's lawyer does mainly conveyancing and you have a complex insurance dispute, then you would need to look further afield. Here are Three of the Best ways of finding a lawyer and what to think about when you do.

1. LAW SOCIETIES

Each state and territory has a law society or institute. These provide a range of services to their members (the legal profession) and to members of the public, including solicitor referral. Tell them if you have special requirements, such as the location of the practice or a lawyer who speaks a language other than English. You will be referred to a number of firms which practice in the relevant area of law.

Most states also have an accredited specialist scheme. This means that lawyers have applied to be recognised in a field of expertise, such as family, personal injury or property law. The lawyer must have a certain number of years of full-time practice notched up as well as a certain number of years in their area of speciality. The lawyer will have passed exams not only in law but also in communication, problem-solving and client service as set by the law society.

- Law Society of New South Wales:
  www.lawsociety.com.au, (02) 9926 0333
- Law Institute Victoria: www.liv.asn.au, (03) 9607 9311
- Queensland Law Society: www.qls.com.au,
  (07) 3842 5842
- The Law Society of South Australia:
  www.lawsocietysa.asn.au, (08) 8229 0222
- The Law Society of Western Australia:
  www.lawsocietywa.asn.au, (08) 9322 7877
- The Law Society of Tasmania:
  www.taslawsociety.asn.au, (03) 6234 4133
- The Law Society of the ACT: www.lawsocact.asn.au,
  (02) 6247 5700
- Law Society Northern Territory:
  www.lawsocnt.asn.au, (08) 8981 5104

2. WHAT IF YOU CAN'T AFFORD A LAWYER?

Legal aid, pro bono, community legal centres and self-representation are all options if you need professional help but can't afford to pay for it.

Advice from **Legal Aid** does not involve means-testing and is free. You can get information, referral to other services and advice over the phone. Sometimes that will be enough and you won't need a lawyer.

If you do need legal representation you will have to make an application for Legal Aid. In most cases you will have to pay a contribution to the costs involved, depending on the type of case you need help with, your financial situation and the merits of your case. Legal aid takes on family and criminal law matters but not commercial or taxation law. Services vary from state to state.

- NSW: www.legalaid.nsw.gov.au, 1300 888 529
- Vic: www.legalaid.vic.gov.au, 1800 677 402
- Qld: www.legalaid.qld.gov.au, 1300 651 188
- SA: www.lsc.sa.gov.au, 1300 366 424
- WA: www.legalaid.wa.gov.au, 1300 650 579
- Tas: www.legalaid.tas.gov.au, 1300 366 611
- ACT: www.legalaid.canberra.gov.au, 1300 654 314
- NT: www.ntla.nt.gov.au, 1800 019 343

Pro bono is when a lawyer acts free of charge or at a reduced cost for the public good. Your law society has a discretionary pro bono referral scheme. You will have to fall within the pro bono guidelines (including an assessment of the merits of your case), be means-tested and have already been refused legal aid.

Community legal centres can arrange court representation, advice and referrals to other services. Contact the National Association of Community Legal Centres at www.naclc.org.au or (02) 9264 9595.

Self-representation means you go it alone. Some courts have a duty solicitor to help people organise themselves for their hearing; this might be limited to procedural rather than legal information. You should contact the registry of the court you will be appearing before to see what, if anything, is on offer. Some courts — like family courts, local courts or the Administrative Appeals Tribunal — are more used to people representing themselves than other courts.

If you are flying solo you could contact your community legal centre or legal aid office for advice. The Australasian Legal Information Institute (www.austlii.edu.au) has legislation, court decisions and other useful information online.

3. COSTS, CASH AND COMPLAINTS

It is important that you understand how you will be charged for legal fees. Generally your lawyer must tell you in writing about all legal costs you must pay. In other words, you must be given a costs agreement and a statement of your rights. If the lawyer is not able to spell out exactly what the costs will be then she must tell you the basis for calculating the costs (possibly an hourly rate) and then give you an estimate. Get your lawyer to put a clause in the agreement that you will be contacted if that estimate is exceeded.

You can make an agreement with your lawyer that you will only pay if you win your case (not in family law or criminal matters) but that understanding should be very clearly set out in writing.

If you are charged more than you agreed to pay or if the costs were not disclosed and they should have been, then talk to the lawyer to resolve the issue. If you are still unhappy, talk to the legal service commissioner or law society in your state or territory.

If you agree that a part of the bill is right then pay that part.

If a lawyer is holding money for you, perhaps after a successful court judgment, then this money should be held in a trust account with an approved institution such as a bank or building society. The law societies monitor the records for trust money.

ON SPOUSAL MAINTENANCE

1. WHAT IS IT?

Spousal maintenance is financial support paid by one spouse to another because one of them cannot adequately provide for themselves. Both husbands and wives have an equal duty to support the other. Maintenance might be made by periodic payments or in a lump sum. If you are in a de facto relationship, spousal maintenance is not covered by the *Family Law Act* and varies from state to state.

2. HOW DO YOU GET IT?

An application for maintenance can be made before or after a divorce, but the application should be made within twelve months of the divorce. The family court has to weigh up the needs of one party (food, clothing, house, car and health expenses) with the ability of the other party to pay for those needs. The Court takes into account your:

- age
- health
- income
- property and other financial resources
- standard of living
- ability to earn and whether the marriage has affected this ability
- care of any children of the marriage.

3. WHEN DOES IT END?

Spousal maintenance ends if you remarry or possibly if you enter into a de facto relationship. In the latter case, the court would look into the financial relationship between you and your defacto in deciding whether you were capable of supporting yourself. Payments automatically end on the death of the payer.

APPEARING IN COURT WITHOUT A LAWYER

1. GETTING READY

Get your documents organised so you can refer to them quickly. If you have a large number of them, put them in coloured folders according to subject. It might be useful to have them in date order. You will need a book for note-taking and pens.

If you are going solo, you might want to organise for a friend or a support person to come with you. They can enter the courtroom with you and sit at the back. People under 18 may not be allowed in the court, so if you have younger children you will have to make other arrangements for them.

You should dress in a way that makes you feel confident in the courtroom environment, for example in a suit. The judge will usually be wearing a gown and wig, and any lawyers will be dressed professionally for work.

2. IN THE COURTROOM

Aim to get to court early so you can watch some other proceedings from the back. Don't forget to turn off your mobile phone. When you arrive, give your name to the court officer and let that person know that you are appearing without a lawyer (unrepresented). You can ask the court officer any other question relevant to the day's proceedings, such as whether your case is before a judge, magistrate or other judicial officer, which will determine how you address the person who is sitting on the bench (at the front of the room): a judge or magistrate is 'Your Honour'. Once you know who you are appearing before, write down the term of address at the top of your notebook.

When you enter and leave the courtroom it is usual to pause at the door, face whoever is sitting on the bench and nod your head.

You might have to wait for your case to be called because there will be a list of other matters. This is a good time to study how the court runs and take deep, calming breaths.

When your case is called, move from the back section of the courtroom to the bar table, which is usually two tables in front of the bench. The other side and their lawyer will also be at the bar table. It is usual to stand up when you are speaking to the judge or when the judge is speaking to you. When the judge is speaking to the other side or speaking generally, you can sit down.

Don't put any food or bags on the bar table. Only use the table for your writing materials.

The judge will understand that you are representing yourself and that this makes a stressful situation even more difficult, but you are bound by the same obligations as someone who has a lawyer. If the judge says something to you that you don't understand, ask politely for an explanation. Make notes as you go; in particular, write down any orders that the judge makes. The court will mail you a copy in due course.

If the judge reserves (holds over the decision to allow time to think about it), you will be told what date and time to come back to court to hear the orders. On that same day you will get a copy of the orders and the reasons for them. If the judge leaves the bench after your matter, stand and wait for the judge to leave the room.

3. SAFETY IN THE COURT

This is particularly relevant in the family court. If you fear for your safety in attending court or any counselling sessions, you should tell the court in advance. Bags and personal belongings are checked when you arrive at the family court. The court can make arrangements to protect you so call 1300 352 000 if you have concerns. Some registries have safe rooms or separate entry points or video facilities. If you suddenly feel threatened when you arrive at court, tell the court officer immediately.

DISSIPATING THE HATE AGAINST YOUR EX

1. Take up an activity that encourages venting, such as boxing or the drums.
2. Focus on success, not revenge: aim to be happier and fitter.
3. Get out of the house, talk to people and, if you need to, talk to a professional.

ON DOMESTIC VIOLENCE

Domestic violence is physical, verbal, emotional, sexual and/or economic abuse by a family member to another family member or members. It is more common than you probably think with nearly a quarter of women across all cultures and economic and age groups who have been in a relationship experiencing violence. What can you do?

1. SUPPORT

If you know someone who is in an abusive relationship, the best offer you can make is one of support. It is not interfering to offer to talk or help someone who is being abused: it is a public issue, not a private one. Your support is important whether the person being abused decides to escape from the relationship or remain in it.

2. COUNSELLING

You can ring a community health centre, family support centre or women's health centre for counselling. The telephone numbers for these centres in each state are in the front of your telephone book. A national and confidential helpline for Violence against Women — Australia Says No can be contacted 24 hours a day on 1800 200 526.

3. LEGAL PROTECTION

The police can tell you how to take out a restraining order or Apprehended Violence Order, the aim of which is to protect you from violence or threats of violence made by a spouse, an ex-partner, a de facto partner, a parent or a child by forbidding them to do certain things.

ON RELATIONSHIP DEBT

1. WHAT IS IT?

It is common for a woman to guarantee a child's loan (going guarantor) or to open a joint loan account with a partner (co-borrower). Both of these commitments are known as relationship debts. We enter into these financial arrangements because we value the emotional relationship but haven't necessarily given a lot of thought to the legal responsibilities. You should think about the financial relationship as if you were entering into it for the benefit of a stranger. In other words, read all the documents carefully, ask questions and make sure you understand the answers. Don't sign a document you don't understand. If you feel uncomfortable or pressured into signing a document, that probably means you shouldn't sign it. If you do sign a document, keep copies of all the paperwork and a finger on the pulse of the ongoing financial situation by reading the regular statements from the lender. Get legal advice about what your obligations will be in the best- and worst-case scenarios.

Remember: the relationship may not work out but the financial obligations are ongoing.

2. GOING GUARANTOR

By going guarantor you are promising to repay a loan if the borrower is not able to do so themselves, so the lender will come after you to recover the money. This is no small commitment.

If you decide to go guarantor you'll sign a contract of guarantee. The law requires that a contract of guarantee contain a warning notice advising you to read the contract as well as an information statement that the lender must give you prior to you signing. The lender must also give you a copy of the credit contract which sets out what is being borrowed and the charges.

Make sure that you understand the amount of money needed to pay off the loan, how much has already been paid off and whether any amounts owing under the contract are overdue. It is not easy to withdraw from going guarantor so you must be very certain that you want to go down that road.

The loan may be for a set sum (a loan for your husband's business) or it might be ongoing (your boyfriend's credit card). In the case of continuing credit, put a limit on the credit and so confine your liability to paying back only that amount of the loan. You must have told the lender in writing that there is a limit. You may also have to sign a security agreement. This is a legal document in which you are putting up something of value as security, such as your house.

If the borrower defaults or fails to pay under the loan contract then the lender will usually get a judgment debt (the amount outstanding plus interest and costs) from the court against the borrower. If the borrower is bankrupt or has gone missing, then action to recover the money will be taken against you as guarantor. This could involve your house, your car or your wages.

3. BEING A CO-BORROWER

You are a co-borrower if you take out a loan with your partner in joint names, meaning that you are both responsible for debt repayment. It is one thing to borrow money for your joint use so that you will have a share in whatever you are borrowing money for. But if you are a co-borrower and the loan is to the advantage of your partner only then you should think very carefully before going on with the financial arrangement. You will be responsible for the whole debt if the wheels fall off. There is no legal requirement for you to sign a loan document just because your partner wants to enter into a loan. If you are the highest income earner then it would of course make more sense for the lender to go to you for debt repayment if something went wrong.

If you separate from your partner, write to the lender and ask that the joint account be frozen or closed until you have had an opportunity to work out your financial settlement. Just because you are divorced or separated does not mean that the lender will not pursue you for your former partner's debts.

AT THE POLICE STATION

1. THE ARREST

You can be arrested if the police have reasonable cause to believe that you have committed an offence, or are about to commit an offence, or they have a warrant for your arrest.

If you are under arrest, the police should tell you that and why you are being arrested. It's not a good idea to physically struggle or have an argument with the arresting officer. If you do, the police are allowed to use as much force as is necessary. If the police use unreasonable force to make the arrest, that is assault. If you are unhappy with the way you are treated, make a note of the police officers' numbers on their uniform.

If you are under arrest then resisting is an offence, and the police could charge you with that even if you are innocent of other charges. Sitting down on the ground is not resisting arrest. Once under arrest, the police can hold you for a maximum of four hours (unless you are suspected of being a terrorist) or must apply for a warrant for an additional eight hours.

If you are not under arrest you do not have to go with the police. You can't be arrested for questioning but the police may ask you to go with them to the police station to assist enquiries. If you are not under arrest and don't want to go with the police then you don't have to. Always speak to the police as you would to your grandmother, politely and clearly.

2. THE SEARCH

The police can search you if they have reasonable grounds to believe that you are carrying out some illegal activity, have stolen items, are carrying prohibited drugs or plants or you are in possession of a dangerous item, such as a weapon. In those circumstances the police could pat you down, look in your handbag, search your car or scan you with a metal detector.

If you are being searched, the police officer must tell you his or her name and why you are being searched.

3. THE STATION

If you are arrested and taken to a police station, you have a bundle of rights that the police should tell you about. You have the right to remain silent, which means you don't have to answer any questions that are put to you. You do have to give your name, address and date of birth. If the arrest arises from a car accident, you do have to give details of what has happened.

You have the right to ring a solicitor, friend or family member. You also have the right to have that person with you while you are being interviewed.

The police will ordinarily make an electronic recording of the interview. You do not have to answer any questions. You might be fingerprinted or photographed for identification purposes. If the charges are later dropped or you are acquitted, you can ask that the photographs and fingerprints be destroyed.

If you have been charged with an offence that is not considered serious (something other than robbery or other violent crime), you will be released from the police station on bail. The decision as to whether or not you will be granted bail is made by the officer in charge of the police station. You probably won't get bail if you have previously committed an offence while on bail or have in the past failed to appear in court.

AT THE DOCTORS

1. WHAT IS INFORMED CONSENT?

Making a decision about your medical treatment after being given all the necessary information to make that decision is called informed consent. Most of the time, medical treatment can't be given until you have given informed consent. You may be asked to sign a consent form.

Informed consent includes telling you about potential risks, benefits, the cost and alternative treatments. Risk is the one that most people worry about. The upshot is that it is important to ask lots of questions so you know exactly what treatment is being undertaken and the doctor knows what kind of information to give you for you to make an informed decision. The greater the risk of harm, the greater the need to ask lots of questions and the greater the obligation on the doctor to give information.

If you are not happy with the explanation, you have a right to ask more questions or get a second opinion from another doctor.

2. CAN I GET HOLD OF MY MEDICAL RECORDS?

Your doctor or hospital must give you access to any of your medical records that were collected after 21 December 2001. You can get access to information before that date if the information is being used or disclosed by your doctor.

Access might mean looking over your records, taking a copy of those records with you or having them explained to you. You might be charged a reasonable fee for providing the information.

You are also entitled to reports or letters written by another health professional, for example, from a specialist to your GP, even if that document is marked 'in confidence'.

3. WHAT ARE MY RIGHTS AND CAN I COMPLAIN?

As a health consumer you have a right to:

- satisfactory service
- dignity and privacy
- adequate information
- due skill
- treatment in a professional manner
- the right to redress if these measures aren't met.

If you are unhappy with your medical treatment your first response should be to speak to the doctor; put your concerns in writing or make an appointment to see them. If you see the doctor in person you should make file notes of what was said immediately after the meeting. If you have been treated in a hospital, the hospital will have a social worker or patient representative who could be your first point of contact.

If you are still dissatisfied you can contact the health care complaints commission in your state or territory:

- NSW: Health Care Complaints Commission, 1800 043 159
- Vic: Office of the Health Services Commissioner, 1800 136 066

- Qld: Health Quality and Complaints Commission, 1800 077 308
- SA: Health and Community Services Complaints Commissioner, 1800 232 007
- WA: Office of Health Review, 1800 813 583
- Tas: Health Complaints Commissioner, 1800 001 170
- ACT: Health Services Commissioner, (02) 6205 2222
- NT: Health and Community Services Complaints Commission, 1800 806 380

You also have the option of bringing a civil action against a doctor for damages. This is a serious step. You will have to be able to prove that the doctor was negligent, and that the negligence caused you injury and you have suffered as a result. You will need legal help to run this sort of claim.

AT THE SHOPS

Here are Three of the Best of your rights when you are shopping.

1. WARRANTIES

Warranties come in two forms and you need to understand both of them to be an effective consumer. First up there are implied warranties, or warranties under statute, which give you a number of basic rights. So the goods you purchase must be:

- Of 'merchantable' quality, which means that they must meet the standard of quality and performance that you would expect, taking into account their price and description. If the goods are being sold because they are seconds or damaged it should be made clear.
- Fit for a particular purpose if you made that purpose known to the person who sold them to you.
- A match for any description or sample that relates to the goods. If the package your goods came in showed a picture of the goods and gave a description of what was inside the package, that is what you should get.

If any of these warranties are broken then you are able to return the goods and get a refund. These warranties can't be avoided or changed by the shop. A sign at the cash register which tries to waive away these rights is of no effect. If you forget to send in a manufacturer's warranty card the rights still apply. A shop can't fob you off to the manufacturer if there is a problem under an implied warranty unless that is a preferred course of action.

It is very important that you keep the receipt or proof of purchase. Try to get into the habit of keeping your receipts in a file, preferably labelled for each month. That way you can find them when checking your monthly credit card statements or if you need them for refunds or exchanges.

The second kind of warranty is a voluntary warranty, and these go beyond the ones set up by law. A shop, for the sake of reputation and good customer service, might say you can bring a pair of shoes back within a week if you decide you don't like the colour. You are not relying on a statutory warranty to return the shoes; they are of merchantable quality, it is simply that you have changed your mind. If the shop has told you about this kind of warranty then they have to stick by it.

2. REFUNDS

If the shoes you bought aren't of merchantable quality or fit for purpose, you can ask for a refund of your money when you return them. So if the shoes have a basic fault that you didn't know about when you bought them, or don't do the job that you believed they would do relying on the shop's advice, or don't match the sample that you were shown, or don't fit the description of the shoe on the packaging, then you can ask for a refund.

You won't generally be entitled to a refund because you have changed your mind about the goods (those shoes really are the wrong colour), or you knew the goods had a fault when you bought them, or you haven't got the proof of purchase and the shop can't tell if they are their shoes, or you have damaged the shoes by not following care instructions or by mishandling.

So if you want to be in the strongest possible position before you return the shoes, ring the shop up as soon as possible and tell them about the problem, make a file note of that conversation, return the shoes to the store with the proof of purchase promptly and make sure the shoes have not been used or further damaged in any way.

If the shop has a sign at the cash register, or anywhere else in the shop, which says 'Choose carefully – no refund given' or 'We are happy to exchange or give a credit note but we don't refund' in relation to normal stock, then you can ignore it. These signs are illegal.

As to refunds of deposits, make sure you have a good understanding with the seller, preferably in writing, as to what will happen to a deposit if you don't proceed with the purchase.

If you can't arrive at a fair outcome with the shop over a refund you can contact the office of fair trading or consumer affairs in your state. Have a look at 'Consumer complaint' on page 391 for how to go about it.

3. LAY-BY

Unlike using a credit or store card, there are no credit charges when you buy on lay-by. When you put goods on lay-by you are entering into an agreement with the seller to pay a deposit and then pay the outstanding balance by regular instalments. When the goods are entirely paid off you get to take them home.

Make sure you understand the paperwork that goes with the contract. The lay-by statement should set out: the purchase price of the goods, the deposit paid and the balance outstanding, the dates on which the instalments are due to be paid, the cancellation charge and the date of the final payment. Cancellation charges vary but the Australian Retailers Association recommends an amount of $25 to $30. If you are late for a payment the seller can cancel the agreement after notifying you and giving you at least seven days to make payment.

CONSUMER COMPLAINT

When you consider how many purchases and trade dealings you undertake every week, most of the time your life as a consumer is trouble-free. It is, however, your right to complain about poor service or faulty products, so this is the Three of the Best approach if you are not a happy shopper.

1. YOUR RIGHTS

It is important to know your rights as a consumer (see 'At the shops' on page 387) so that if you are unhappy with goods or services you can calmly and confidently approach the seller with your grievance.

As a first step, go to see the seller in person and explain what you believe the problem is.

If you get nowhere, write a letter to the owner, manager or customer service department of the seller. Set out what goods or services you have purchased, on what date and in what circumstances. Explain what you are unhappy about and how you think the matter should be resolved. For example, the goods need to be repaired and, if that is not possible, returned to the store at no cost to you. If you are unsure how to rectify the problem, ask the seller to suggest a way forward. After all it is their reputation on the line. Give the seller a reasonable time to reply to your request but state that if you have not heard by the deadline you will be taking the matter to the relevant industry body.

Keep a copy of the letter you send and make sure you keep the tax invoice or sales receipt.

2. MAKING A COMPLAINT

If you are being ignored or not getting satisfactory answers from the seller within a reasonable time frame, the next step is to make a complaint to the relevant industry body. Some service providers such as lawyers, doctors and architects, have their own internal complaint systems.

If you are unsure who to take your complaint to then call the office of fair trading or consumer affairs in your state. Generally, and it does vary from state to state, these agencies can help with complaints relating to:

- goods and services
- property and tenancy
- motor vehicles
- door-to-door selling
- second-hand dealers
- product safety
- domestic building works
- refunds and lay-bys
- false advertising
- consumer credit.

It is worthwhile looking at the website of the agency in your state for information, including online complaint forms. Generally these agencies can negotiate on your behalf and perhaps arrange some form of dispute resolution, but they don't have the power to make the seller fix your problem.

- NSW: Office of Fair Trading, 133 220, www.fairtrading.nsw.gov.au
- Vic: Consumer Affairs Victoria, 1300 558 181, www.consumer.vic.gov.au
- Qld: Office of Fair Trading, 13 13 04, www.consumer.qld.gov.au
- SA: Office of Consumer and Business Affairs, (08) 8204 9777, www.ocba.sa.gov.au
- WA: Consumer Protection Division, Department of Consumer and Employment Protection, 1300 304 054 www.docep.wa.gov.au
- Tas: Consumer Affairs and Fair Trading, 1300 654 499, www.consumer.tas.gov.au
- ACT: Office of Fair Trading, (02) 6207 0400, www.fairtrading.act.gov.au
- NT: Consumer Affairs, 1800 019 319, www.consumeraffairs.nt.gov.au

3. MAKING A CLAIM

If the relevant agency can't sort out your problem you need to consider whether to go to the next level. Each state and territory has a small claims tribunal or court which has the power, if the evidence supports it, to make a variety of orders, including that the supplier or you: pay money, return goods, repair goods, rectify services, pay damages, or vary or cancel a contract.

The advantage of these tribunals or courts is that you are allowed to represent yourself, thus keeping costs to a minimum. To prepare you will have to organise all your paperwork, preferably in date order, and have multiple copies ready for the other side and the person hearing the claim.

Generally you will register your attendance on arriving at the tribunal and then be called when it is your turn. You will be given time to speak, call witnesses or hand up affidavits (a sworn statement by a witness). You will be asked questions by the person hearing the claim and the other side. It's a good idea to watch a few cases before you appear yourself to get a feel for how the tribunal operates. At the end of it all you will get a result; whether it is the one you wanted is another question.

The websites of each of the relevant tribunals or courts can give you tips about appearing and how to prepare for it, the likely costs involved and the sort of orders that could be made.

- NSW: NSW Consumer, Trader and Tenancy Tribunal, 1300 135 399, www.cttt.nsw.gov.au
- Vic: Victorian Civil and Administrative Tribunal, 1800 133 055, www.vcat.vic.gov.au

- Qld: Small Claims Tribunal, (07) 3247 4578, www.justice.qld.gov.au
- SA: Magistrates Court, (08) 8204 2444, www.courts.sa.gov.au
- WA: Magistrates Court, (08) 9425 2222, www.magistratescourt.wa.gov.au
- Tas: Magistrates Court (Minor Civil Claims), (03) 6233 3623, www.courts.tas.gov.au
- ACT: Magistrates Court (Small Claims Court), (02) 6217 4272, www.courts.act.gov.au
- NT: Local Court (Small Claims Jurisdiction), (08) 8999 6225, www.nt.gov.au/justice/ntmc/small_claims

ON YOUR PRIVACY RIGHTS

We are constantly handing out information about ourselves to organisations and government agencies, but what are your legal rights?

1. GATHERING

If an organisation is collecting information then they need to tell you a few things, such as who they are and how to contact them, why they are collecting information, the consequences if you don't give them the information, how you can gain access to the information they will hold about you and, most importantly, what other organisations they might give your information to.

This information might be in a written document or the organisation might tell you about it verbally. Make sure you understand it and, if you don't, ask questions. If the organisation is asking about things that you just don't see could be relevant to the business at hand, ask more questions. If you are still not sure of your position, contact the Office of the Privacy Commissioner on 1300 363 992 or look at www.privacy.gov.au.

Information is sought from you over the phone, in person, in surveys, over the internet and by mail, and we all probably give out more than we need to because we are so used to living in the information age. So don't be too relaxed with your personal details. If you are throwing out printed material, shred it first. If you are discarding old plastic cards, cut them up. Check that you are in a secure website before giving personal information online.

2. ACCESS

Once an organisation has information about you it is possible to get access to it. There are exceptions to this but, generally, information collected after 21 December 2001 is available to you on request. One way of accessing that information might be to look at the organisation's records and make notes, or you can put in a request for copies. If you are having difficulty getting access to an organisation, contact the Office of the Privacy Commissioner as above. The organisation might charge a fee to give you the information you are after.

3. STORAGE

There is no fixed 'life span' for the information you give an organisation. If the organisation no longer needs the information then it should be destroyed. If it is out of date then you can ask that it be changed so that the records being held about you are accurate. You should put your request in writing and ask for confirmation that the update has been done.

ON YOUR CREDIT FILE

1. DEFAULT

If you owe money and 60 days have passed since your payment was due, then a default can be listed on your credit file. The creditor (the person/organisation you owe money to) must have written to you asking for payment of the outstanding amount before that can happen. Credit reporting agencies hold information about loan applications, late payments and defaults. Subscribers can check your credit worthiness through these agencies.

2. PAYMENT

A credit reporting agency does not have to take your overdue payment off your credit file once it has been paid. An agency must, however, attach a note to your file saying you have paid off the debt once it has been advised of that by you or the creditor. When five years have passed since the debt was reported, the credit reporting agency must remove the debt from your file (if it was a 'serious credit infringement' then it can be on file for seven years).

3. ACCESS

Contact Veda Advantage (Australia's largest credit reporting agency) at www.mycreditfile.com.au for a copy of your credit report. If your credit listing is not correct, contact the Office of the Privacy Commissioner on 1300 363 992 (www.privacy.gov.au).

AFTER SEXUAL ASSAULT

1. REPORTING

You are the only person who can decide whether to proceed with making a complaint to the police. You will need to think about whether you want to give evidence about what happened to you or, alternatively, how you would feel if no action is taken against the person who assaulted you. Another consideration is that in some states a complaint to the police is necessary before you can apply for victim's compensation.

You should have a medical examination as soon as possible after the assault. Don't change your clothes or shower beforehand.

Even if you don't want the police to take the case to court you can still report the assault. This is an informal report and it may help the police in their investigation of other sexual assaults.

2. INTERVIEWING

If you decide to go ahead with reporting the sexual assault you will be interviewed by a police officer who will type up a statement of all the events before, during and after the assault. You can request to be interviewed by a female officer. The police should take all steps to safeguard your privacy, but you will be asked difficult questions. Your statement may be videotaped or audiotaped as well as written down. You must read the statement and make sure you agree with it before you sign it. Make sure you get a copy of your statement. You will also be given a victim card with your investigating officer's name, the database number of your case and details of victims' support services.

You can talk to a rape crisis centre while you are at the police station or afterwards. You can have a support person with you or ask the police to take you to the nearest sexual assault service or hospital.

3. IMPORTANT CONTACTS

- NSW: Rape Crisis Centre, (02) 9819 7357, 1800 424 017, www.nswrapecrisis.com.au
- Vic: CASA Forum (Centre Against Sexual Assault), (03) 9635 3610, 1800 806 292, www.casa.org.au
- Qld: Brisbane Sexual Assault Service, (07) 3636 5206, 1800 010 120
  www.health.qld.gov.au/violence/sexual/services
- SA: Yarrow Place Rape and Sexual Assault Service, (08) 8226 8777, 1800 817 421,
  www.yarrowplace.sa.gov.au
- WA: Sexual Assault Resource Centre, (08) 9340 1828, 1800 199 888,
  www.kemh.health.wa.gov.au/services/sarc

- Tas: Sexual Assault Support Service, (03) 6231 1817, www.sass.org.au
- ACT: Canberra Rape Crisis Centre, (02) 6247 2525, www.rapecrisis.org.au
- NT: Sexual Assault Referrral Centre, (08) 8922 7156 www.health.nt.gov.au/Children_Youth_and_Families/ Sexual_Assault_Referral_Centre

INDEX